Relation

A COLLECTION OF MATERIAL

FROM WRITING WORKSHOPS IN

SCHOOLS WITH CHILDREN OF ALL AGES.

By

Ian Blackman

Contact the writer at:

ianblackman66@gmail.com

Dedication

To my son, James [who changed his name to Electra Von Metalhead the 7th] who I hope will find peace, love, and happiness.

INDEX.

PART ONE.

Page

PART TWO.

A YOUNG GIRL'S QUESTIONING OF LOVE

It was a spring morning as the young girl sat staring out of a classroom window.

'Right,' said the teacher, 'Today we are going to watch a video.'

Whoopee thought the young girl, I love videos.

The teacher continued, 'It's a video made specially for you all and it comes under the heading of sex education.

The young girl tried to hide her blushing cheeks but she wanted to know, and had often wanted to ask all sorts of questions but never found the courage to ask. The half-hour video raised even more questions in her mind and the young girl was determined not to feel embarrassed and to ask these questions not in school, but rather in the safety of her own home, alone with her mother. She thought she understood what grown-ups did with no clothes on and she felt she understood why. She understood that it was important to love someone and be loved, to make the thingies of sexual intercourse a natural way to love each other. What she didn't understand was how you knew when you really loved someone and this was the first question she asked her mother, when arriving home. The young girl noticed her mother's eyes open a little wider, a split-second surprise, then a kind smile.

Her mother thought then answered, 'It can take time to love someone, although some people believe in love at first sight.'

The young girl said, 'You mean the very first time you meet someone you can fall in love with them?'

'Yes,' replied her mother, 'Although I must admit I haven't heard of very many.'

1

'Did you and dad?'
'No, quite the opposite, we didn't like each other that much at first.'
'Why?'
'Well, we were in a crowd of friends but gradually we grew to like each other.'
'Then you got married.'
'I said 'like'- there is a huge difference between like and love.'
'How different?'
'Well, if you think a most natural thing for many is to marry and have children, watch them grow-up, see them hopefully have children, then as a couple you are alone again but much older, your love hopefully having grown stronger.'
'So, it takes time to love someone?'
'Yes, it can do but you need to be with them in all kinds of situations, when you are happy, sad, angry.'
'I've seen you and dad get angry.'
'I would say it's more upset than angry.'
'Why?'
'Well, people are different and it isn't always the case that two people who are in love can agree on everything. You see it's all about compromising.'
'What does that mean exactly?'
'Well, sometimes doing what someone else wants, sometimes giving in.'
'But why would you do what you don't want to do?'
'Because sometimes people want to do different things at different times, like I might want to stay in and snuggle up with your dad and watch a film, while your dad might want to do something else.'
'So, who wins?'
'It's not a case of winning- I'll go with him and do whatever he wants, then another time we may stay in and watch

2

a film- it's about sharing as well as having your own time to yourself.'

'But how do you know when to do what dad wants, and what you want?'

'Ah well, that's when you have to be careful- many people fall into the trap that because they love someone, that someone can take advantage of that person's love.'

'Like our neighbour Mrs Perkins when her husband comes back from the pub drunk every night.'

'How do you know that young lady?'

'I hear her sometimes while I'm in bed and her shouting.'

'Yes, I know and you see, they, if asked, could say they love each other and in a way, they may do, but we are talking about a loving relationship when each other brings out the best in each other.'

'Do you do your best for dad?'

'I try but it's difficult showing your love all the time, when sometimes you are tired, sometimes especially when raising you and your younger brother, we don't get a lot of time, but we try and talk and that helps us- you must always find time to talk about how you feel. If you are made to feel like a nuisance then you've not met the right partner.'

'So, love should help?'

'Yes, it shouldn't be a nuisance that you care for someone- it shouldn't cause problems but saying that, love sometimes can.'

'Why?'

'Well, people can get jealous or get so frightened of losing the other person they can try and put a cage around their partner, it's called being possessive.'

'But if they love them?'

'It's not as easy as that I'm afraid, because not everyone can be in control of their feelings. Love can do strange things to a person.'

'Like Mrs Perkins and her drunk husband.'

'Some people don't know perhaps how to love, whilst others are too frightened to love because in their past maybe they have been let down and hurt.'

'So, love can hurt?'

'Oh yes if you are willing to open your heart to someone you must be aware of the possibility of getting hurt.'

'But why?'

'Because people aren't always what they seem and also one person's love in a relationship can be stronger than the other.'

'How?'

'Well, some people fall in love quickly, some take longer, whilst others may never fall in love.'

'Never? But that's sad.'

'Yes, it is, sometimes it's because they've never meet the right one?'

'How do you know who the right one is?'

'Good question, I think we've all got some idea of the kind of person we would want to spend the rest of our life's with but there is a big problem.'

'What's that?'

'Well, your ideal man, [if he exists?] you want to give your love to, may be different when you're 16, 26, or 36. Now it would be nice to know that you meet a boy at 16, fall in love and as you grow, he grows and if your outlooks change you will still love each other.'

'But why should people change?'

'Everyone grows not just in their bodies but in their minds emotionally. That's what maturing means. People mature at different speeds and it is widely thought that girls begin maturing at a younger age than boys.'

'I know that, some of the boys in my class are so childish.'

'But you mustn't grow up too fast, your childhood only happens once.'

'You look worried mum?'

4

'Well, I have always hoped you would feel comfortable talking to me about everything?'

'Yes?'

'Well, what worries me is that innocence is so precious, but by you asking all these questions and all the education on sex....'

'Yes?'

'Well, I find it difficult to know how much to tell you and at what age?'

'But mum I'm no longer a child.'

'Well, when I talk about love I wonder if at your age, it is possible for you to get anywhere near the feeling you have when one is in love?'

'But I love you and dad and I know how that feels.'

'Yes, that's a good feeling and it's a family love.'

'And I love my brother.... sometimes!'

'Yes.'

'And my best friend I love.'

'I know but when you have a boyfriend you may begin to feel a different kind of love.'

'But isn't love the same all the time?'

'Well, it should have the same feelings of respect, of being a friend, of being a good and loyal person.'

'But there is more is there?'

'Yes, because the most wonderful thing that can happen to you when you fall in love is that your boyfriend loves you as much as you do him.'

'And then we will be alright?'

'Yes, but it will help a lot if you both can talk to each other.'

'Talk?'

'Yes, because another dangerous trap lurking is that sometimes people say things like I love you, then their actions, the way they treat someone shows they can't really love that someone.'

'Like Mr and Mrs Perkins.'

5

'Perhaps.'

'So mum, why doesn't Mrs Perkins tell him?'

'Perhaps she's not bothered or frightened of him?'

'But that's terrible.'

'But you must be aware of what can go wrong, then if you have a good man, you will be able to talk with him.'

'What? About feelings?'

'Yes, it is important you feel comfortable talking to your boyfriend or friend about feelings, about emotions, and do you know what is a GOOD TEST to know whether they care for you?'

'What?'

'If someone upsets you, they will listen to you and not keep saying you are being silly. If they think you are being silly wanting to talk about things that you don't think are silly, then they don't understand you or perhaps they don't want to understand you- this applies to all friends not just a boyfriend.'

'Dad understands you, doesn't he?'

'Yes, I feel he does because the important thing he is willing to listen and luckily for me he tries to understand how I feel- sometimes he can't because I can't always describe how I feel or why something upsets me, but I do try and of course it works both ways when he is upset or has a problem. This is true friendship because you share problems not only to do with us but with work etc.'

'So, love is also sharing.'

'Yes, and so is friendship.'

'So, love is friendship.'

'Yes, and an understanding of how important it is to never take for granted the love given to you.'

'I never will.'

'I hope not because many people do- people can treat each other very badly, sometimes even cruelly.'

'So much to know mum.'

'Yes, and also some people don't want to get married to the first person they fall in love with.'
'Why not?'
'Because they want to experience life first, see the world.'
'But they could do it together?'
'Yes, they could but this is the sad thing about love- you see, love is always tested I think.'
'What do you mean?'
'Well, if the love is strong enough, if it is a true love then people will still stay together.'
'And if it's not true love?'
'Then often people part but sadly it can happen that one person loses their love for someone.'
'But how?' Why?'
'It just happens in life and it can make you wonder if it was love in the first place?'
'What else could it be?'
'There's an old saying that talks about the head and the heart. Your heart says one thing when the head says something else.'
'How do you mean?'
'Well, your heart could be bursting with love for someone but your head tells you something is not quite right, that something is wrong.'
'Wrong?'
'Well, you don't know why you love this person?'
'But don't you love because you want to love?'
'Yes, but it's nice if you are loved back.'
'So why mum would your heart say one thing and your head another?'
'Because it can take a long time to get to know someone, and to make things even more confusing sometimes people don't know who they are, or can't find the words to express how they feel.'

7

'I'm still confused mum- why if two people love each other why shouldn't it last forever?'

'Because as I said people change, can change- it would be so simple if we all never changed- so you meet a boy, fall in love and this person you love never changes.'

'But why would he change if he loved you?'

'He may love you forever- but he may meet someone else or want to travel or you may drift apart.'

'But I wouldn't want him to.'

'But you can't possibly know what will happen in the future, you can only be aware of what could happen and so protect what you have, that's why it's important to talk.'

'But if we are right for each other, we will stay together forever.'

'I would like to think so but people can be careless and what I am trying to tell you is life isn't always that simple and people can make mistakes.'

'What do you mean fall out of love?'

'Yes, and then realise they really did love that person, and then in other instances people wonder why they loved someone.'

'Why?'

'Because like Mrs Perkins she must wonder if or why she still loves her husband? Sometimes people stay together because there is nothing else or they are frightened of being alone or sometimes they choose to ignore they are in a bad marriage.'

'That's sad mum.'

'It just depends if you are lucky enough to meet someone who shares your hopes, your understandings about love.'

'Like you and dad.'

'Yes, but it hasn't been easy- everyone has their ups and downs and disagreements but you learn to compromise and try and come to some sort of agreement. Sometimes you

8

must give in and the problem is to know when and what to give in to.'

'How do you mean?'

'Well, take Mrs Perkins- in a truly loving relationship first Mr Perkins wouldn't go down the pub every night and leave his wife at home- it should never get to that situation whatever the problem is between the two of them. It should have been sorted out by talking it through. But some people hope the problem will go away or they ignore it and some people can't talk about their feelings.'

'Why not?'

'I've said before they sometimes really don't know how they feel or they can't find the words or right words to describe how they feel.'

'Dad can, can't he?'

Yes, but when I first knew him, I had to nearly force him to tell me how he felt about things.'

'Why?'

'Because he hadn't been used to talking about his feelings. He was brought up in a family where they didn't talk much about feelings.'

'What did they talk about?'

'Well, everything except I suppose.'

'So, dad was like that.'

'Yes, but it took time but I used to say to him how important it was to talk and also if he wanted to get to know me, we must talk, not just about the weather, work, or what and when or where we went, but to talk about us, each other and what we wanted from life, from our relationship.'

'Did dad have trouble in finding the words?

'Yes, but luckily for me he began to see that men were wrong not to talk about how they truly felt- it can be dangerous to keep everything inside of you- it's far better to share your feelings with someone you can trust.'

'I remember telling some boys that I had seen my dad crying at a film and they made fun of it.'

'Yes, that's it- men in the past were brought up to act strong and to be in control of their emotions and never to show too many feelings.'

'So why are we different mum?'

'Well, I feel sometimes we women are more capable of being the most natural of the two species.'

'I'm glad I'm going to be a woman.'

'I only hope you do meet a good man who won't be any trouble.'

'So do I, I want to fall in love, get married and have children.'

'Yes, I hope so too and that you will still be in love at 60.'

'So, when I fall in love, I will love like you and dad.'

'Yes, in a way but it will only be the start of you learning how good love can be, and over the years how it can become something that makes you stronger, gives you freedom and helps you grow as a person but still keeping you together with your partner, because you both choose to be together. You will be able to share your time together, have fun, have sad times, have time on your own, have time together and what keeps you together is the feelings you have for each other that as you get older, the love becomes deeper and deeper.'

'What about condoms?'

'Pardon?'

'The video we watched today mentioned about condoms for safe sex?'

'Well, I think that perhaps should be a subject for another day under a different heading.'

'What do you mean?'

'Well, some people don't always have sex when they're in love and I would prefer it that you only have the one belief- that you only have sex when you have got to know each

other and are both in love and realise what a powerful and wonderful act it is to show someone you love and care for them by making love.'
'You mean sex mum?'
'Yes…Loving sex.'

THE TALK I NEVER HAD

[Around the age of eleven my father told me sometime we will need to have a talk about the facts of life and my sister close by said I probably knew all about it… but I didn't, and I waited and waited but the talk never happened.]

'Right son I think it's time you and I had a talk.'
'Dad… whatever I've done wrong I'm sorry.'
'No, you haven't done anything wrong… I hope?'
'It isn't about men trying to give the cat a grade one haircut is it?'
'No that was years ago son, now you're older I felt…'
'Is it something important?'
'Yes, it is.'
'Football?'
'No look, listen now, don't interrupt.'
'Sorry dad.'
'I wonder how much you know about the opposite sex?'
'You mean girls?'
'Yes.'
'Lots.'
'What do you mean lots.'
'Lots, I know lots.'
'Like what?'
'Well, they're only after one thing.'
'What's that?'
'You know.'
'No, I'm asking you.'
'Well, what's in your trouser pockets.'
'I beg your pardon.'
'Sweets, only joking.'

'Look son, I think we need to have a serious talk.'

'Okay dad.'

'About…about…sex.'

'Oh that, I know all about that.'

'And where have you found out about that?'

'We talk about it at school.'

'Who with?'

'Me mates.'

'And what have they to say on the subject of sex?'

'That it's done when two people love each other.'

'Good, good, what else?'

'That you must be careful of catching diseases so it's best to wear a condom.'

'Yes right, anything more?'

'That being… I think they said…faithful shows you really love someone.'

'Good, it seems you have things in a nutshell so to speak.'

'No, not quite dad…there's something I'm not sure of though?'

'O what's that?'

'Well, what is love?'

'Go ask your mum.'

'Mum what's love?'

'Go ask your dad.'

'Dad, mum says ask you.'

'Go back and ask your mum properly.'

'Mum, I've got to ask you properly what love is?'

'Well okay, let's look it up in the dictionary…ah here we are…Love…to have a great attachment to, and affection for. In other words, it should be something meaningful.'

'Can I take a look mum…but look it also says…to have passionate desire, longings and feelings for.'

'Yes, that's right- that's where love is shown in a physical way.'

'You mean sex?'

'Yes, it's another way for two people to show their love for one another.'

'But mum, on a soap episode I saw what's her name spend the night with a bloke and then they ignored each other the very next day?'

'Sex should be something special between two people like an act of trust.'

'But mum, there's a girl in the sixth form who has different boyfriends all the time.'

'How do you know that?'

'Reliable sources.'

'How do you know it's not mere gossip or a boasting of the ego?'

'What do you mean by ego mum?'

'Let's look it up…ego…the self of an individual person- a conscious thinking subject.'

'So what?'

'Well, you must make a conscious decision whether to have sex with someone because you truly love them or because you just want to…'

''Want to what mum?'

'Well, treat sex as a bit of fun I suppose.'

'But mum I thought I saw…here let me look up love again…yes look- a deep feeling of sexual attraction and desire.'

'Yes, in a loving way.'

'So mum, what happens if I don't feel enough love for a person?'

'Then you don't have sex with them.'

'But mum, one meaning of sex it says here is…feelings or behaviour resulting from the urge to gratify the sexual instinct.'

'Sometimes I wish I hadn't encouraged you to question so much.'

'So mum, you can have sex to please yourself without having feelings.'

'Well, I suppose some people do, but believe me it is so much better if the feelings are heightened by being with someone you love and who loves you.'

'But mum how would you know this unless you first have sex?'

'By listening to what other people say- I have told you lovemaking is another way of showing your love for someone.'

'So, it's wrong to have sex if you don't love them?'

'Yes, I think so.'

'Even if they want sex and don't love you.'

'Where do you get all these thoughts from?'

'Everywhere.'

'All your dad and I can do is to tell you what we feel, and hope you will meet someone, experience falling in love, get married maybe, have children maybe, and stay in love with that person you trust your mind and body to.'

'And meanwhile mum, I can have sex, can I?'

SIXTEEN DAYS FROM A DIARY OF A SIXTEEN-YEAR-OLD GIRL

SATURDAY.

Secret diary under lock and mattress, I don't know if I should be angry or not? Tonight, in one moment of madness I forgot everything I had learned about dealing with sex. My first time wrapped in NO words... he didn't say, 'If you love me you would sleep with me.' He didn't say, 'You're sixteen, you should have done it by now.' And why did I have no words? Why didn't I tell him I wasn't ready? Why couldn't I tell him that when it feels right for me, I do want him to be the one, the first one, perhaps the only one?

Instead, I let him direct his erection towards the inner sanctum of me, of who I am, and I'm so angry cos I gave in, cos I thought I might lose him so I let him do it and now the moments lost. I saw the candlelight, I felt the feelings inside me, I knew I'd be scared of the moment. I felt his kisses soft on my body. I held him close and felt as one. But all is gone- lost in a mixture of feelings. Could he possibly know what I write now? Perhaps IF it had been his first time, he may have got closer to knowing my feelings but then perhaps not.

Dear diary- I feel I pleased him but not me. I did it for him. Can't you see diary somethings you can give freely and somethings you give dearly- the price I had to pay today...

SUNDAY.

I talked with my friend who said she couldn't wait to get her first time over and done with- she made me feel old-fashioned, prim and proper. I couldn't stop her asking me what I thought? I told her I hoped the next time would feel right. I couldn't tell her that for me sex was far more serious than that. I tell you diary I could do without the soft music, the candlelight, if I could definitely have the feeling that I wanted him inside my heart. If others can change partners frequently, I can't.

Why do friends make me feel so old fashioned? I know they might not understand that I want the passion, want the love BUT I must be IN love, am convinced I am right.

He has not rung and I wonder if he's with someone else tonight? Suddenly, I don't feel so sure I am right? Perhaps he is waiting for me to ring? Perhaps he's too embarrassed to ring because he could feel it had not been right for him or me? I hear people change, grow apart. They say at 16 I have a lot of growing-up to do, yet who I sleep with I want it to be that we stay together forever.

MONDAY.

I saw him at school and he said hello as if I wasn't there. I must admit thinking, if Saturday night had been THAT good, he should be happy to see me- was it not as good as he made out? I hear other voices shout, 'A good lay.' Why do they say this? Out of boasting, bravado or is it to cover over the fact they've never experienced sex with love? Those few seconds when it seemed he forced himself to say hello told me he wasn't embarrassed. Was it showing me he'd won, got what he aimed for? Was it game, next one please?

I have spent the whole day trying to find less cynical reasons for his actions. Perhaps he covered up his embarrassment, perhaps he thought I thought his actions wrong on Saturday. Talk yes, we must talk. I did look for him after school and have spent most of the evening switching on and off the phone. Somehow, I must be strong-

I must hold on to my beliefs that I must be with someone who cares for me.

TUESDAY.

He wasn't at school today so I phoned him. He sounded very strange on the phone- said it was because he was ill. I told him I'd go round but he said he didn't want me to catch what he had. I couldn't tell him I wanted to talk to him- more worried about him.

WEDNESDAY.

He came back to school today and finally I got to speak with him. He seemed distant, and when I told him I needed to talk he asked what about? He appeared so uneasy with me.

I waited after school but he didn't appear. Rang him and asked him what the matter was, then the bombshell...I can only tell YOU diary what he said. As difficult as it is to write with tears streaming down my cheeks... Yes, he said it...He didn't want to see me anymore- said he was seeing someone else. He said last Saturday he was going to tell me but...

So, what do I feel now... HATE? ANGER? BETRAYAL? No, I feel cheapened, cheapened by his lack of guts to save me these feelings I have now. How I hate those older people's words, 'I TOLD YOU SO.' But diary you don't tell me that- you let me look back and see my mistakes- you tell me he wasn't right for me and that the next one will be, must be.

THURSDAY.

Read my diary for yesterday and felt what a load of twaddle. Trying to convince myself he meant nothing to me- trying to deceive myself I won't be hardened by him. I

HATE MALES- I don't want anything to do with them- they are nothing but trouble.

FRIDAY.

Got asked out today- he heard I had broken-up and wondered if I would go out with him. Gary his name is, very good-looking. YES, I thought, I'LL SHOW HIM. I can get one over on him. I'll show him I can find a good friend who wants me for who I am and NOT for what he can get. I will be very careful- I will go at my own pace. If Gary cares for me, I could say all the things to him I say to you diary? He will understand me if he truly cares for me.

SATURDAY.

Had a really good evening. I must admit I was worried how I would feel being with someone else, but Gary was nice and we talked a lot, and I felt he was interested in ME. When we talked about friendships, I said I only wanted friendship- I couldn't give more. He understood and seemed concerned and I admit diary that now I feel he could be one of those types that are good with words who knew the right things to say and the right time to say them. I felt I knew Gary more than the person I slept with a week ago. Could I have learnt so much in a week? Is it possible to admit I didn't really know him? Tonight, with Gary I listened to myself and realised I was able to say how I really felt- thank you diary- I feel I must thank you for helping. I don't always like what I show you- I am sometimes terrified anyone else will read this- it sounds sometimes silly the way I call you diary but I feel partly a fool for what happened last Saturday, and now no longer a virgin I must somehow put it under the huge hurtful heading of 'experience.'

SUNDAY.

Saw Gary again today, we went for a walk- he never tried to hold my hand or get anywhere near kissing me. Perhaps, he's one of those who takes his time as well? Perhaps, he doesn't fancy me that way? HELP diary, doubts are creeping in. Am I attractive? Am I fun to be with? Don't be stupid! – my friends like me. But do I act? Am I being ME? Or do I do all this to fit into the cluster of much needed friends? I think of my friends I no longer see much because their time, my time is taken up with boyfriends. Thinking about it I don't really see them much on their own.

Anyway, back to today- I shouldn't allow it to worry me if Gary doesn't try anything- I don't want to make the mistake of trying to get him to like me. Perhaps that was the trouble with my last relationship? Because I needed to know that someone liked me, found me attractive, liked being with me- did I give him some sign or signs that I wanted more? No, we talked...or did we? There I go again- yes, we talked about sport, school, films, music, what we should do, when we should meet, but we never ever talked about us. Ah yes, of course, I didn't want to upset him- he never did like talking about us, me, himself- said his dad never talked much. We were having fun so why talk much? Why spoil it by being too serious, and so blindly I came to the other Saturday night when I was so desperate to please him but not myself. What good advice that is eh? I can't quite believe I got myself into that situation anyway- we were both a little drunk- great party and it just seemed to drift into an empty house, into kissing and then I didn't want him to stop but then I did want him to stop and he said, or I thought he said, he loved me. Oh, I know it sounds so naff and weak and stupid but that moment when I knew what would happen- I believed in him OR wanted to believe him- I trusted him but now look at me, how naïve I was- whoever

20

warned me about this? Do others ever talk about this or am I being TOO sensitive? Am I going mad writing this?

MONDAY.

Gary thanked me for Saturday and I must admit a bubble popped up in my head spelling C R E E P but then I saw my old boyfriend- saw him standing confident with his arm around her and I thought PIG, RAT the lot. It really bugged me to think that by his look he felt he'd won the game he played with me- he had triumphed in his conquest and now his next match with her, poor her with naivety in her eyes. Am I a BITCH diary? Am I becoming bitter? I fell for his patter, his charm whatever, like I'm sure many others will do but I thought I would have been different- I really thought it was as simple as trusting in someone and believing they would have your best interests at heart- wow what a load of rubbish-what absolute nonsense.

I say let this be proved to me- if I can't get a boyfriend who merits six tens' then he's failed- I expect only the best- I wish a boyfriend not perfect but as close as one can humanly get. That's it, that's what I'll do- I'll be casual-control my emotions and go nice and slow- I won't be pressurised by friends, whoever, to go all the way- I'll do it in my time. If I get it wrong again, I'll ask why? I'll think of the questions I need to ask. I'll work out what his answers tell me about him, about us, and myself. HELP diary I'm sounding like some courtroom judge and jury! Do I really know how someone should treat me? How do I know if I treat people well? What are my expectations? Oh, it all seems so confusing- I'm too tired diary.

TUESDAY.

Had this strange dream last night- I was in a meadow when the boy I lost my virginity to came to me crying and begging me to take him back, and I said yes but found

21

myself feeling nothing and when he kissed me and asked me if we could continue where we had left off, I said yes. We laid down amongst the wild flowers and all I could do was stare at his face as he lay over me- I felt nothing. I watched him moving on top of me- I felt nothing. When he suddenly opened his eyes, and saw me staring at him… he stopped moving when he saw I was expressionless- I still stared at him feeling nothing. He rolled off me, pulled up his trousers and I saw he felt nothing.

WEDNESDAY.

I hate myself for my honesty-I realise I am lonely and need someone- call it the rebound- how I hate that word rebound. Decided to cool it off for a while with Gary- he was very understanding, too understanding, I think? I must admit again to thinking why didn't he try and persuade me to see him? I want to know someone wants me but I want to be sure, I want that someone for the right reasons. Where are we taught these reasons or is it just a case of find out for yourself and store the learning process under experience? Isn't there an easier way? Yes, marry the first boy you meet- this is how stupid I am now thinking so I'll end diary.

THURSDAY.

Went out with the girls to the club. It was strange but suddenly I felt older than the rest- seemed to have changed since that Saturday- I no longer agreed with their laughter on sex. I knew if I said anything they would think me bitter and twisted. Knew if I tried to explain how I felt they'd not understand, maybe laugh. What am I doing with people like this? I sometimes wish I didn't feel like this- would be much simpler if I just got on with my life without much thinking- just go through the motions- keep myself to my feelings, just have a laugh not get too serious BUT STOP…listen to me diary…I WANT A BOYFRIEND, I want to share

22

moments with a boy who likes me, treats me kindly, with respect- I know how much I have to give. Oh, now I sound too grown-up don't I diary? But I've decided I'm not going to settle with what I consider to be second best, even if it means having no boyfriend!

FRIDAY.

It's funny you know diary- time alone gives you time to think- sometimes too much time to think- I think I'm thinking too much. I should just let things happen naturally. No- that's right, let things happen naturally but be able to say NO- No I'm not sure, No I'm not ready, no feeling guilty, no, if you respect me, you'll listen. RESPECT- what a word diary- what do I know about respect? Two weeks ago, I didn't really know the word existed. Now I say it and wonder how you determine what respect is? How do you decide what is respectful and what is not? My body is my own so I shouldn't let it be used, abused unless I say so, but then how do I know I'm not being stubborn or selfish or even too cautious?

Do I respect other people? Do I respect their wishes? Do I treat others how I expect to be treated? Oh, diary I think I'm going crazy- I think sometimes I tell you too much. If I'm honest, all I expect or hope for, is to love and be loved and to know this love stands a chance of lasting forever. I've read all the romantic books and mags- I've seen the films, lived the hope- surely, it's not all made up? Surely it happens? Yet when I think on my parents, other parents, they never look like they are in love? I never see them kiss much or hug each other, never see them hold hands. Perhaps they do all this in their bedrooms? When I've talked to my mother, she says things can get in the way when married, like life, work, and children. She tells me I am young and free from responsibilities and how sharing a life can present many difficulties. But I don't want life to get in the way or to alter the feelings I have for someone- why get married if you know life will get in the way? Fine if you have no children- you can bore each other to death. Ah diary…now we're coming to the truth- children. Am I obsessed with the thought of everlasting love because I wouldn't want my children to see 'my parent's eyes for each other' in mine and my husband's eyes? I think I'm growing up far too quickly yet I think I needed to grow up fast. I still remember that dream in the meadow when I felt nothing. I wonder if at this moment there are millions of people all over this world feeling nothing?

SATURDAY.

Feels strange staying in on a Saturday night- I wonder what is happening at the club? And who is getting off with who? And how many find a back-seat, a field, a bed, a sofa to feel something? Am I so different from other people? My parents think it's strange I'm not going out tonight- my mother asked if something was wrong? I'd like to tell her everything but I can't, never could. Oh, I am grateful for the love and security she's given me but I just can't tell her about the past two weeks- where would I start? Perhaps I should keep this diary open on my bed and go out leaving the bedroom door wide open.

I've been listening to the same music I listened to when I was with him- I am ashamed to say, despite all I've written these past two weeks, I DO miss him. I can't blame him for everything however much I try. Part of me feels we could start again and this time I'd call the tune. Then there's part of me that remembers how I felt nothing for myself, but all for him. But isn't that what feelings are all about? Giving like a Christmas present without expecting one back? No, I don't think so- you give first and if you don't receive anything worthwhile, then you find someone who will give you a meaningful relationship. Heavy stuff eh diary? Too heavy? I still think I'm going slightly mad and I don't know where all this is coming from and whether it all makes sense? Does it? I'll sleep on it.

SUNDAY.

Feel a little better- had some sleep but reading back the past two weeks I'm confused whether what I feel is wrong or the right way to feel? I mean I keep getting back to the same question…what is the right way to be treated? And if I made a list of rights and wrongs, would they be different from another person's list? I know we are all meant to be different but surely there must be some items on each person's list that are the same? But then I get confused when I think that someone's idea of respect may be different from mine- that my idea of love maybe too wet, too lovey-dovey for some people? I remember watching a programme on battered wives and not understanding how they, a woman, a mother could have him back? How she with swollen lips, black eyes, could still say she loved him and thought he could change or at least hoped he could change especially if he said he would. How she said he knew he had done wrong; he just didn't know what he was doing and was sorry. I wonder if I could put up with this? If I walked out would that mean her love was much stronger and deeper than my love at 16 because she stayed? Or has this thinking just been forced upon me? I'm not sure diary if you are doing me any good? I think perhaps I should maybe stop writing and start living my life…

THE FOLLOWING POEMS

INSPIRED FROM DISCUSSIONS IN WRITING

WORKSHOPS IN SCHOOLS.

She makes me question my idea of love
When she says she loves him and needs him
Yet if a man came into her life and excited her,
Romanced her,
She would leave the love she has now…
But what love is this?
A familiar need?

She makes me question my ideal love
When he thinks he knows her
Yet at moments in their day
This her thinks of the other man
The one who excites her in a way she misses…
Is this deception?
Or an understanding of love,
That however much you are in love
It is not worth sacrificing this love that could
Grow, and grow forever.
It is not worth risking ending this chance
When an attraction elsewhere could come to nothing.
Is this maturity?
That we all meet others that we are attracted to?
Most women imagine but don't touch
Many men touch and can forget.

She makes me question her love
When I think about trust
And the sharing of problems
And how hurt is every part of love

But most importantly
Trust
Trust that your lover is honest with you
Tells you all
So, you can decide what to do…
Not to leave it to touch or smell of infidelity.

She makes me question myself
And in questioning
I discover nothing
But the feeling to be in love
And how I as a man
Can learn from women
Who flirt with thoughts
But take it no further
Because they know the consequences
The risk of losing
The trust.

PAIN.

He opened out his pain
Confiding that he did not know what to do
And as the scene unwound
I saw this 14-year-old boy
Drowning in emotions from the heart...
It had all started well.
Got to know each other
Gradually sharing secret feelings
As meeting by meeting
They grew closer, felt closer together
And then it happened...
Her words like an arrow between his shoulder blades...
Whoever prepared him for this?
Who could ever prepare anyone for this?
She undid all her feelings, all her words to him
By saying, 'Forget all I said,
Every word, forget it...I didn't mean them.'
He stares at me
And I look away from his tears close to falling.
I tell him face her, tell her how you feel.
'I tried,' he said, 'But she doesn't want to know.'
Ask her where do you stand?
'I can't,' he said, 'She may finish it all.'
Give her time then, keep away.
'If I do,' he said, 'She may get used to me not being
there.'
Then ring her.
'She doesn't want me to ring her.'
Feeling it is all over I keep this to myself while I tell him
try and prepare yourself,
If she doesn't want you then free yourself with time,

Free yourself so you can meet someone who appreciates you,
Wants to be with you.
'But she's special,' he says, 'Out of all the girls I've ever met she is by far the best,
I may never meet anyone like her.'
You mean she's one in a million?
'Yes,' he says.
I think on about the millions who never met 'that one for them'
Millions who then must settle for second best?
Perhaps she's too immature?
Perhaps you're asking too much of a 14-year-old girl?
Perhaps she's just panicking because of her strong emotions?
Perhaps she doesn't want the responsibility of a boyfriend?
Perhaps she just wants to be free, have fun, no attachments?
He looks at me…I know this is not what he wants to hear,
Because he wants, and needs the whole thing.
'She thinks I've got too heavy,' he says.
Feelings are not always balanced, I say, often one feels more than the other.
'Yes,' he says, 'I don't want to go running after her, she could walk all over me.'
YOU must decide, I say.
'But what if it were you?' He asks.
I'd finish with her, I say.
'I know,' he says, 'But it's difficult.'

SHE ASKED ME.

She asked me if I could ever be married?
Yes, I said, anything is possible.
And what about your track record with commitment?
Yes, I said, everything can change.

She asked me if I believed it was possible to love forever?
Yes, I said, possibly one per cent achieve this.
And what of you? Could you love forever?
Yes, I said, physically one hundred per cent.

She asked me how could I be so sure?
Because I know what works for me, I said.
And last for your whole sex life?
Yes, I said, if my partner shares the pleasure.

She told me she could never see herself married to me.
Who knows, I said, anything is possible.
But we are so different, want different things, she said.
Yes, I said, but between two people it's all to do with
everything can change...
A kind of understanding,
An understanding that works,
And with this everything can change,
And the most important things are fulfilled...
Being loved, cared for, one's soul being understood,
With this extraordinary understanding anyone,
Anything and everything can change...
Only the look in the eye
The expression
The lips,
The whole bodies sway
Will show if its...
Stay or stray?

BLIND LOVE.

For the first few months
I saw him every night
Then it dwindled to three times a week,
When my friends began to talk
Their word against his…was he a cheat?
I'd ring him
Ask when could we meet?
Don't know, he'd say
So, I played him at his own game,
Don't care anyway, I'd say…
We went our own way.
HE WAS BEING A PIG
I know, but…
He's my first love,
The best boyfriend I've ever had.
BUT YOU COULD DO BETTER
Perhaps…but
I can't have him,
He's got another girlfriend now
But there's always the chance
He could finish with her
It's exciting
This waiting
Perhaps he will
Perhaps he won't.
THERE'S PLENTY MORE FISH IN THE SEA.
I know, but…
I don't want to see anyone else
I don't wish to get serious anyway.
I must get over him.
DOES HE DESERVE ANOTHER CHANCE?
I know it could be better next time around
I know we would have learnt from our mistakes

If it didn't work then I'd know.
BUT WILL HE EVER CHANGE?
Don't know, but…
I feel so lost without him
So alone
I wish I could phone
And tell him.
WHY CAN'T YOU RING HIM?
I just…can't
Lots of times
I think it
Plan it
I just can't
I just can't say it.
BUT HE COULD BE THINKING THE SAME?
I know, but…
I'm frightened of the truth
I need my dreams
First love never dies
You know!
GO MEET PEOPLE, GO TO A DISCO
I used to go with him
GO TO THE PUB
We first met in a pub
YOU MUST GO OUT
Yes, I know but…
I'm just not ready yet
YOU KNOW YOU'RE BEING BLIND
I know, but…
It's these feelings
They won't go
I remember our good times
I need time
Lots of time
I want him…back.

DOWN TOWN.

Saturday morning
Holding
Hands around town.
He's mine
I'm his
We're one.
As one we meet two
Of my friends…
Don't flirt
Don't hurt me.
You're mine.
We hear shouts…
His mates
He hesitates.
A twitch in my hand
But he doesn't let go.
And I know
He's proud of me.
We walk past
A window full of marriage.
He stops
He looks
And smiles.

NOT WISHING TO BE HERE.
[AIDS Test Results]

Ignoring totally the one-way signs,
The white arrows pointing on tarmac…
I meet a car full-on,
I'm scorned at… irresponsible?
I don't really care, I smile, cover my eyes.
Two women smile back
I point two fingers to my head
Admitting fault,
Then, park my place in a hospital slot.
I don't wish to be here!
No-one in my family ever went through this.
I would prefer to do nothing…
Anything…than be here.
I'd prefer, honestly, not to know at least for the next few
years…
Perhaps never know until
In a room somewhere a doctor tells me
I have AIDS.
So now sitting in my comfortable car seat
Waiting my turn, fully conscious that in thirty minutes
I'll walk into that hospital, my future health-free,
Wanting as much chance to
Die naturally, as you and me
But oh…how my heart beats fast
Last…last…please last.

STIRRING UP THE PAST.

After half-a-dozen beers,
In his leather jacket in a heavy rock pub
He tells me he's going away…
Four days in Devon…
With the lads, riding the dare-devil surf!
'Dangerous,' he says,
'Could face death,' I say,
'Yes,' he says polishing off another pint.
And moving across to his teenage fiancée
I stir up my past to ask…
'Wouldn't you like to be with him in his last moments?'
'Yes,' she said,
'No,' he said.
'I understand your side,' I say looking at him, 'It's an
adventure,
But the romantic side is being together.'
'Thank-you,' she says, 'I'm glad you see my side.'
I stop stirring my past
When I see how easily it mingles
With his present.

TIE BREAK.

With new balls
The middle-aged teenager,
Spring in his step…
Discovers
Sex.

Stretching into late night hours
The fresh-faced innocence
Commences the game…
FOOT FAULT
DOUBLE FAULT…
He's nervous,
Never been in this position before.
His biggest catch so far was a match on video…
She was gorgeous… dry lipped him mad.
She was all hot flushes.
If he had possessed an ace, he would have given her one.

With used balls
The sweat clad teenager
Tingling…
Uncovers
Sex.

ALL I WANTED WAS SOME CONDOMS.

I felt unperturbed
With all I heard
About being served
By a young lady
In a chemist.
All I wanted was some condoms...
Just ask...
No need to think long and hard about it
Get straight to the point...
'Please miss, I wish to buy some condoms,
Can you recommend any?'
Does she blush to make me feel embarrassed?
Do people turn open-mouthed to make me feel
uncomfortable?

'Please miss do you have any testers; you know like you
have with perfume?'
Do her eyes open wider to make me feel as if I were
asking for the world?

'I like the look of this packet but what are the condoms
like?
Can I try one on?
Can I get it out?
Have you got a changing room?'
Why does she look at me that way?
Would she really want her customers to see a condom-
covered thumb?
Is it my fault I've never used one before?

DIFFERENT TIMES.

She puts her work away in the wardrobe
Chooses what to wear for the evening.
And makes time for a long soak,
Washes her hair,
And as her weekend face goes on
She dreams a dream
About her man.
Later that evening
They meet.
Their eyes meet.
She knows.
He knows.
They both have the same wish…
But the actual duration of this wish
Resembled the time it took them to get ready…
She three hours
He three minutes.

URGING ME INSTEAD.

She said to me
She wanted to be
A virgin
When she's wed.

She said to me
She wished to see
A virgin
Share her bed.

I said to her
Could we confer
Urging
Me instead.

AH HA!

My mate James
Has a thick black food-catching moustache,
Dark curly hair,
'It wasn't me' eyes,
Round face,
And he's
A bullshitter.
He's been telling me
He's been doing nothing with her…
Just friends
End of it he says.
But I knew different
The day
His top lip appeared.

SENSITIVE?

Walking through town
Checking out the faces
I try to live their moments of passion,
Romance, a cuddle here, a kiss there,
And going deeper
I feel their disappointments
And then the thought...
Perhaps there aren't enough good partners around?
Second best for most is all they ever meet...
Some make the most of it
Others turn off
Switch on to a family
Get what one can from a job
Some find the courage to get out
Be on their own
Waiting perhaps for something better
Something always hoped for,
Always felt existed...
Some wait forever.

Walking through town
Instead of looking up
I look down.

UNTITLED.

Should my idea of love
Be that of yours?
As if my tree shed no leaves
And stirred not whilst strong winds moved all around.

Should my view of love
Be that of yours?
As if my sea wavered no more
And dared not lap a shore that once shared a tide.
No!
Spare me my idea of love
That my dreams can be shared
For my very soul lays vulnerable enough
With cruel, heartless sentiments all around
That underly the very essence of love.

IN CATHERDRAL GARDENS.
[observing an elderly couple.]

Some forty years of marriage sit close apart…
She eyeing a sparrow searching for scraps,
He feeling the young man's hand stroking her long black
stockinged legs.

The afternoon sun altering the green of grass…
She breathing the holy, early summer air,
He scheming sensations next move.

The clouds queue up heavy and grey…
She organising the next few minutes to the car,
He fumbling for reasons to stay.

NOTHING CHANGES.
[over a game of ping pong.]

Over table tennis she tells me about her new man and how
she's wanting commitment…
Is disappointed, hurt by his cold cool attitude.
I tell her he may be frightened of commitment; he may
have been badly hurt,
He may even be the type of man who is emotionally
immature?
Continuing our game…she's losing…too many aggressive
unforced errors…
'It's always me who makes up after our quarrels, it is me
who wants to see him more,
I have given everything, even my pride but still he is
unsure.'
I tell her you can't force it out of him, you can't expect to
change him, and perhaps he
May not be honest, open enough with you? [Why hasn't
he told his 'ex' all about you.?]
And then I send over the net a cunningly disguised vicious
spin that she never reads and
She's lost the game...but fair game she's up to play
another…with herself…she has been
Damaged [more damaged than maybe she realises?] She
ignores her self-esteem, her
Need to be loved respectfully, thoughtfully, with
sensitivity, and I don't even go into
Talking about her parents [one meeting was enough
information], her childhood, I see it
In her body language, her answers…her lack of answers.
I change to using my weaker hand, and she beats
me…just.
But she won't change her choice of man, consistently
choosing the wrong type of man,

Consistently getting hurt, disappointed [unaware of levels? Ranging from a loser to the best].

Tears…Tears walking in the park alone, pain because he can't explain what he wants [have your cake and eat it?].

Does he want casual sex?

Does he want commitment?

She knows all this deep down inside, but her tears say something else…

Beaten to LOVE…match over, whitewashed, physically drained…

New date next week,

Clean sheet…

Same old story [settling for second best?].

GOOD LOOKING.

And she meets this fella…
First date and he buys her a slap-up meal,
Orders the best wine,
And when he drives her home,
Latest model,
He doesn't much like it when at her door…
She turns and says, 'I'm not ready for the rest,
Good night and thank you for a lovely evening.'

Walking back to his car he feels like
Asking for his money back.

A NAMELESS TEACHER.

I saw do-dar the other day
You know…thingarmebob
The bloke who eloped with watchermacallit,
Oh, what was her name…
Married the dustbin man…
Lived next door to Fanny Anne,
Was a fan of oojimaflip
That chap who passed away just the other day,
You know…thingamajig
Desperate Dan the actor man,
Played alongside flybernite
In thingummy's film…
You know thingy…
Oh whatsisname!!!

You should see me at school
When reports are due!!!
I never have a clue…

UNBELIEVABLE.

I'm always late
And how I hate to see
My teacher's jaw gyrate,
As he yells at me...
'I suppose you have another unbelievable excuse as to
why you're late!
Let me see what could it be this time?
You thought today was Saturday?
Your bedroom door disappeared?
You thought the school had moved?
You helped an elderly person across the road...twenty
times oh no we've
Already had that one, haven't we?
No, don't tell me, let me guess, it's good for the
imagination...
You foiled a bank robbery, took on the gang single-
handed, beat them up,
Nicked them, spent the reward money, and still managed
to get to school by 9.30!
No, I'll calm down and have one more guess...
You got out of bed the wrong side and fell out the
window? Punctured tyre,
Punctured foot that's why you're wearing only one shoe,
alarm clock stopped,
Parents didn't wake up, you got run over by a bus, fell
down a drain, walked into a tree,
Wet yourself? Oh, stop nodding no boy! Just tell me then!'
'My baby died Sir.'
'Your baby?'
'Yes Sir.'
'But it's physically impossible for you to have a baby,
boy!'
'My furry baby Sir.'

48

'Oh, please don't tell me there's another one like you on its way here to terrorise us?'

'No Sir, it's my guinea pig.'

'Oh, your guinea pig, what happened?

'Got squashed Sir.'

'Squashed! By what?'

'A foot Sir.'

'Whose foot?'

'My foot.'

'Your foot?'

'Yes Sir, you see, I was determined to prove to you that I could get to school on time

So, I set my alarm clock an hour earlier.'

'So, what's that got to do with your guinea pig?'

'Well Sir, I couldn't set the guinea pig's body-clock, could I? I mean it's impossible.'

'So?'

'Well, I got up, got dressed, put my shoes on, went charging down the... and SQUELCH,

Poor Freddie was coming up to see me at his usual time, I'd trained him to do that Sir...

He never stood a chance...so I had to bury him with my shoe Sir!'

MY PARENTS REALLY ARE...

My parents really are boring.
They never, ever go out.
Me mum knits, me dad sits snoring,
And they tell me not to doss about!

My parents really are a dead loss.
They never want to go on holiday.
I do try to argue the toss,
But still, they won't go away.
No chance for me to be alone,
At home,
With booze...
And my girlfriend!

My parents really are a pain.
They always say my music's too loud.
And then they drive ME insane
By telling me I'm only allowed
Up till eleven on weekdays
Weekends till midnight...well whoopee!
But it's not fair, it's not right
I want to stay up,
Really late with me mates,
In a house
That's adult free,
So, we can be W I L D!

My parents really are annoying
'The girlfriend' can sit on my bed
And just when we're enjoying
A quick...round the door pokes a head
Saying,
Want a nice cup of tea?

There's a good film on T.V.
What do you two
Find to talk about?
Mum!
Dad!
Just get out
Of
My room
My life
Your house!

EXAMPLES USED IN WORKSHOPS TO GENERATE QUESTIONS/DISCUSSIONS ABOUT RELATIONSHIPS.

LOVE PERSPECTIVES.
[1]

He likens her to a pebble on the shore,
Each new wave lapping closer
Till drawing her into the depths of passion
He says, 'How do you expect me to regard you as special when at any moment
The seagulls cry could deny me any hope of saying you are mine.'
She thought, 'Bout time he said what he thought and she kissed him, lead his hand,
As silently his sex was bought.

QUESTIONS.
[A] In a relationship what could be the consequences of one of the partners coming on too strong?
[B] Do you think you can call your partner yours? Why do some want to possess their partner? Wanting to own them? Is it more the male that shows this?
[C] Do you agree or disagree with the statement that females are the 'catchers'- the more needing to settle down than a male, because the woman is equipped to have the baby and prepare a nest, a homemaking situation?
[D] What do you make of the last line? What is meant by it? [Is it to do with a woman using sex as a weapon?]

[2]

She wanted fun…
He wanted fun…
It was their number one aim.
No blame…they had safe sex six or seven times
Then found another…
They wanted to have fun…
NEXT?

QUESTIONS.
[A] Discuss why you could or could not be attracted to
this attitude?
[B] What could be the consequences of adopting such an
attitude?

[3]

They met when both arrived at 'Big school'
Their innocence remarkably intact they made a pact…
To stay friends until the very end.
Both moved into their teens
Aware of all other distractions, temptations
They held hands and planned for the time…
Their first time…
Her parents empty house, music too risky…
Think of the slammed shut front door?
Seconds needed to look unruffled-unravelled.
They touched each other naked
Having waited for this, now nervous the first kiss, kiss,
kissed, whoops missed.
They did not hear the slowly opened front door,
The tip-toeing up lush carpeted stairs.

They were unprepared for the whipped open bedroom door…
Mother open mouthed- boyfriend turning, daughter covering.
How different it could have been, if this parent had seen,
The young lovers cuddling with the warm afterglow from lovemaking.

QUESTIONS.
[A] If you had been in the parents place how would you have reacted?
[B] Why is it many teenagers find it difficult, sometimes embarrassing, to talk to their parents about personal matters especially sex? Do parents have the right to know you are having sex [or making love? What's the difference?] in your relationship?

[4]

'I didn't have sex until I was married, I made your father wait,' her mother said.
And before the daughter could retaliate…her mother continued, 'Why do you want a physical relationship so young when you've only just turned sixteen?'
'Because I love him,' the daughter replied.
'But you've only known him a year, I knew your father several years before we were married.'
'It just feels right and I want you to know my intentions instead of hiding it and making out sex is something dirty or nasty.'
'Your father and I have a good, healthy sex life but we got to know each other first.'
'But mother you said you made father wait?'
'Well, sometimes men can be in too much of a hurry.'
'How do you know this mother?'

'Through experience.'
'Well mother, I wish to find out through my own experience not yours, perhaps we could then discuss it further.'

QUESTIONS.
[A] Can you discuss how someone knows when it's right to enter into a physical relationship?
[B] How much can you be guided about relationships and how much are you expected to find out through experience?
[C] What could happen if you enter into a sexual relationship too quickly?
[D] Which factors should you bring in when deciding when you are lawfully allowed to have sex?
[E] Do you think the daughter has the right to talk to her mother that way at the end?
[F] Discuss the dialogue that could take place when one of the partners wants sex while the other partner is unsure and would like to wait? What pressures could be exerted?

GOT A QUESTION.

Got a question I need answering…
It's not a clever question and I don't need no clever
answer…
You see it's to do with you and me, yeah that's right- I
wanted to know…
Well, whether…you do a turn? Know what I mean?
What yer looking at me like that for? All I want to know is
if I'm wasting my time?
Barking up the wrong tree-know what I mean? What yer
walking away for?
Just a simple, yes, or no? Oh, too early, is it? Haven't
known you long enough?
Oh yeah, I know all about the respecting business-Don't
try anything for a week-
Getting nearer all the time…to what I'm asking now…I
mean it's stupid playing these
Games, when you could be thinking that you want to do
me and I want to do you-you know- sex, sorry you prefer
making love.
Just imagine us fancying each other like mad and I'm too
afraid to make a move, in case you don't think I respect
you, when all the time you could be thinking how much
you really want me, but must make me wait so I respect
you, and you review it weekly.
IN THE NAME OF SEX, you don't have to worry about
respect- if you let me as early as the first date, I'd respect
you for letting me. If you asked me to love you-I'd still
love you tomorrow.
Come on love, how about it? How about you and me
doing what comes naturally? What yer calling a taxi for?
Oh, I see, it's back to mine or yours yeah?

QUESTIONS.

[A] How would you have dealt with someone like this? What would you say? What can you do if a male doesn't seem to know the word NO? Would it make any difference where you were? Flat? Disco? Pub? What should you be wary of in this situation?

[B] Could you describe how you would know if someone was safe to be alone with?

ONE DREAM TO GIVE HER HOPE.

It's funny to think…at this moment
He doesn't even know me.
It's strange to think…we don't even know
Where we shall meet.
And if you ask me what he will look like
I couldn't say.
And if you told me I will fall in love
With a tall dark sensitive man
I'd laugh who is he? And where can I find him?

It's laughable to think…
There could be thousands of people
Out there
Thinking the same as me.

QUESTIONS.
[**A**] Would it be difficult to admit to having this dream? Is reality far harder?
[**B**] Is it more difficult for women to go out to meet men? As you get older would it become easier or more difficult?
[**C**] Why do so many marriages fail? Is it because the choice was wrong to start with? What can go wrong? What advice would you give in choosing a life-long partner?

THE VERY FIRST TIME/INNOCENCE?

The time and day decided after late night front door moans.

Parents shall be at work…both bunk-off school.

He stood at the bedroom window surveying the cul-de-sac…waiting…

Days ago, in a pub he caused a snooker miscue from the clang-clang of a condom machine.

Nude, still waiting, he feels shy, embarrassed by the thought of putting it on in front of her.

So, standing there he manufactures an erection and rolls it on...Still no sign of her…

Ten minutes now…he feels exhausted…then she appears…front door opened…hello…

Come in he says charging up the stairs holding firm his condom covered erection.

She's a good girlfriend- doesn't ask questions and in seconds asks if he can put it in…

Before it goes down! She nervous, shares his naivety…erection successively inside her…

He laying on top of her…eyeball to eyeball…both stationary!

QUESTIONS.

[A] What pressures are there on a male regarding the first time? Any different if it's the first time for both? Are there more pressures on the male than female?

[B] Who should take responsibilities regarding precautions?

[C] Why could it be a blow for the male if he can't perform? Why could this happen? How could a female help with this situation? How would a female deal with her inexperience? What attitudes could people have if a female was experienced in sex? Is it true if a male has many girlfriends he's labelled 'a lad' while a female could be given not very pleasant adjectives?

[**D**] In which circumstances would you have unprotected sex? Could you trust a partner when not using anything?

HER BEST FRIEND TOLD HER.

She won't listen, can't listen to her best friend's words…
'He's seeing someone else.'
But she still asks him and he says no,
Then he asks who was the accuser?
She says her best friend.
Can't be much of a best friend, he says, to spread false
rumours.
And when her best friend tells her again,
She asks him again, and again he says, no, don't you trust
me?
Yes, she says.
Once more she's told and once more, she asks him,
And he leaves her for her best friend no more.

QUESTIONS.

[A] Why did she not want to believe her best friend?
[B] Does it take courage to ask someone if they ARE
seeing someone else?
[C] How difficult is it to really trust someone? What help
do others give to work out who the cheats and liars are?
[D] How is it you can make such a big mistake when
judging whether someone really is a best friend or friend?
[E] What is the difference between a friend and a best
friend?

61

INFLUENCE.

I catch a glimpse of my family at odd moments in their
life's, my life...
And wonder do we ever have much chance of shaking off
their influences,
To a time when you can confidently say we are ourselves,
When we know what is us, and not them?
Now my family no longer have their say...I think on their
good points and...
Shudder at the rest. Is this disrespecting the dead?
When all the things they said they truly believed.
Had they ever conceived they could have been wrong?
Yes, I miss my family...
But not their negative influences.

QUESTIONS.
[A] Who teaches us to be good parents?
[B] How easy can it be for parents to pass on their
mistakes to their children?
[C] How difficult is it to know when you are young
whether your parents adopt a right or wrong way of
bringing up their children?
[D] Should society, schools, equip the person with the
information to be able to stand a fair chance of becoming a
good parent? What could this information be?
[E] How difficult is it to live by your own standards and
way of thinking, values etc when living with your parents?
Which sort of areas cause the most disagreements between
teenagers and their parents?

CONFORMED.

They conformed beautifully…did what society asked of them.
Covered over the cracks… Outwardly a model marriage, inwardly a sad waste of two
Human life's that could have been enriched by being with someone more suited.
But they took the chance
Unaware of what DID happen…
A morally dead marriage that falsified the fulfilment of two people coming
Together in mind and body to better each other's life…
'Marry when you're young and silly.'

QUESTIONS.
[A] Do people conform to the idea of marriage today? What are the reasons for getting married? When should a couple decide when to get married and when to live together? What are the advantages and disadvantages of both?
[B] Could it help the success of a marriage if couples got married later in life say in their thirties? Why could this help?
[C] What can be the disadvantages of a couple staying together because of the disruption to their children if they seperated? What decisions must you make when deciding to divorce or not, when children are involved?

AN IDEAL?

Closing his erotic novel, he takes a piece of toilet paper to
quickly jot down his
Ideal mate…Huge breasts, slim waist, doesn't talk much,
loves sex, long legs,
Cherry pouting lips, and then he deliberates…?
Would he be able to keep her? Hang onto her? Could he
handle competitive
Looks from hunks? Should he take out an overdraft? No,
she would be faithful,
Loyal and doting…she would enjoy just being with HIM.
But how would he know if she truly loved him? Could he
be with her every minute
Of every day, except moments like this?
He remembered a play he'd seen in which a woman had
played her man the fool
And loved him for what she was getting…scheming Eve?
No match?
On his next piece of paper, the pink blinked at him…Not
so beautiful, more natural,
Shy, homely, motherly, adoring, dependant. A wife
plainly, but friends.

QUESTIONS.
[A] This piece deals with insecurities. Is it based on fear?
If so fear of what?
[B] How important is the physical attraction in a
relationship? Is personality more important than looks?
[C] Do you think some people marry just to get what they
can out of it like money and/or status?
[D] Do you think he is right to go for the list at the end? A
safer list?

SECOND BEST.

She wants a sunset as well as the sex…making love she
prefers to call it.

And shuffling the many faces, mannerisms she encounters,
Her experience concurs…How do I know? How much of a
chance must I take?

Do I give all of me and hope he sees? Or will it be the sad
tale we all know so well?

She wants the lot…the test and knows no reason why she
should settle for second best.

She's seen the deadness, the struggle, the defeat in others.
But she'll not be moved from being loved.

She knows the best places to see a sunset.

QUESTIONS.

[A] Do you think you can be too choosy?

[B] Is second best better than no-one? Are people
pressurised into marriage, if so for what reasons? Is it still
the case that women can feel 'left on the shelf'?

[C] If a partner was not right for your friend would you
tell them? If you had to tell them, how would you tell
them?

[D] How can falling in love affect your choice of partner?

SHE WANTS.

She wants to live in a world where doves need not exist,
Where flowers keep their fragrance through no winters.
On the sofa in her sitting room close to the flames she
moves her hand to his,
Then laughs at her romantic touch of the heart.
She slings on a coat, picks a pub, ignoring the pick-up
negatives,
To unroll a list of reasons with her wine.
Curling about the embers in darkness, she smiles at the
ending of the Flintstones...
Tiny lights in tiny bedroom windows all going out...Were
they that fictional?
She wants the world where she can be herself...part of a
team, and stroking the pillow
Next to her she feels as brave as her first day at school.
And when the morning sings, she sings for she will not
feel love, have love
If it means, only, to have something better than this
loneliness.

QUESTIONS.
[A] What is meant by the pick-up negatives?
[B] Do you think if a male sees a female in a pub on her
own that she is there to be picked up?
[C] What pressures are there to have a boyfriend or
girlfriend?
[D] Do some people use, 'I love you' to get what they
want from a partner?
[E] Do you think many people get married because they
are scared to be alone?
[F] Are people who are not married by 30, 40, 50, thought
of as being strange or sad?

REALITY.

She dislikes the term 'sniffing around' when applied to boys.
She hopes they won't just be interested in her curves but in her mind, her personality
Her wish not to have the rush into bed with all its pleasures. She'll wait, expect him to wait,
And if she loses him, she'll cry like all of you. No, she'll stand her ground, keep her values,
Ignore the 'hard to get' sneers, the labelled 'teaser,' in the hope she'll find the boyfriend of her dreams?
Singing along passionately to the lyrics of a love song
She wonders, when he doesn't ring, has she got it all so wrong?

QUESTIONS.
[A] Is there such a thing as an ideal romantic love?
[B] What sort of pressures are put on teenagers to have sex?
[C] Do some girls still get labelled 'hard to get' or 'tight' if unwilling to have sex early?
[D] If a boy did say he would find someone else to have sex with if you won't, would you leave him? How would being madly in love affect your decision?

1993.

Going back to my teenage, twenties game, learning the
ropes...what works what doesn't,
I laugh at a saying I recently heard...'Dear God make me
good but not yet.'
How I think on these words being right but wrongly
used...
Gaining experience as the hunter, conscience treated to a
holiday on the moon,
And when re-visiting how I sent it to Venus forever.
And now older I feel immaturity is just an excuse,
How I convinced myself, my feelings, that it WAS all fun,
how I was able to play the field,
Daisy chains in the long grass, kisses, and laughs,
Moonlit bathing in pleasure...at leisure
What treasures to remember...
'Dear God make me good but not yet.'

QUESTIONS.
[A] Do you think the person in this piece is being hard on
himself in not allowing immaturity as an excuse? How
much can you get away with by saying you are young or
inexperienced or having a good time etc?
[B] When it says 'learning the ropes, the game,' what do
you think this entails? What can be learned? `

68

NATURAL.

Still remembering the sunshine drying her eyes, as the sea
swallowed her sandcastle,
She peers through her confusion, her added 'bits' to her
body.
She thinks she's sure 'how to do it.' She's heard friends
say it's great, but can hurt.
She tells them she'll not to do it till she's married, and
when they laugh, she wonders
What he'll look like, be like? Will it be in a lane? The
back seat of a car? Or whilst babysitting?
Will she get caught out pregnant like her friend and marry
the father? Or be like her other friend...One-parent
family?
She thinks on diseases...no she'll do it with only one.
Thinks of the daily paper...a couple sharing a virus...no
her man will be a virgin.
Thinks of the boy who told her friend he was a virgin, was
what she wanted to hear...
He wasn't!
Condoms? Like eating a sweet with the paper on he told
her.

QUESTIONS.
[A] When your body develops towards maturity what
emotional changes can take place?
[B] At what age did you feel you knew 'all about it?'
[C] If you became pregnant would you marry the father?
Or if your girlfriend got pregnant, would you offer to
marry her?
[D] Why are there so many one-parent families today? Is
it usually the woman that ends up looking after the child?
In what situation would it be better for the child to be with
just one parent?

UNRUBBERED FEELINGS.

Look, I've seen the ads, the warnings and I think it's just
the governments way of spoiling
My fun…it's an attempt at gaining a more moral society,
but I won't be chained to these
Party-pooper tactics. I'll find a partner who feels the
same… we'll take the chance and
Have what the nineteen-sixties had…free love with all and
sundry. Safe sex? Would you fancy eating…
A sweet with the paper on and miss out on the feel of the
softness of a vagina?
No, I'll go for the pill every time
And her good memory and enjoy that pure
Unrubbered feeling.

QUESTIONS.
[A] In today's climate how selfish or irresponsible is this?
[B] Do you think there are people willing to take a chance
without using any other form of contraception other than
the pill?
[C] What would be the safest form of contraception to
stop pregnancy? [other than not having sex]

THE FOLLOWING MATERIAL INSPIRED BY WORKING IN A PRIMARY SCHOOL WITH ALL AGES.

I am now going to tell you a story about NOTHING…I shall continue my story with SOMETHING…NOTHING'S brother who became EVERYTHING. EVERYTHING was once NOTHING before he became SOMETHING. One day NOTHING was walking along the road when he met SOMETHING, who said to NOTHING, 'Hello how are you?' NOTHING said nothing.
NOTHING continued walking anywhere until he came to somewhere, 'Yes,' said NOTHING, 'I've said something!' and NOTHING turned into SOMETHING and became EVERYTHING!!!

TEASING ALTERNATIVES.

Jack and Jill went up a hill to fetch the milkman's
daughter.
Jill fell down and broke her crown,
And Jack's eyes filled with water.
…….
Two little dickie birds sitting on a wall…
Along came a cat ten feet tall…
No little dickie birds sitting at all!
……
Mary had a little…hippopotamus, its hair was soft as snow
And everywhere that Mary went the hippo had to go…
It followed her to school one day it was against the rule,
And made the children laugh and play…
When it ate their village school!

71

Love is… caring for someone
helping someone
giving them cards
kissing them
walking together
holding hands
being married
Love is… a pram.

Happy is… a red face
blushing
mouth-up.

Sadness is… mouth down
enough tears in your eyes
to last a lifetime.

RIGHT AND WRONG.

Right is when teacher tells you.
Wrong is an upsetting look.
Right is red warm.
Wrong is shivery white.

FRIENDS.

A friend is… someone who likes you a lot
        you like a lot
        to share secrets with
        who you love
        who you play with
        who you hide with
        who helps you
        who helps you do your homework
A friend is… someone who NEVER calls you names.

HALF-JOKING.

I want to be a dead loss. I want to work with hic-ups. I
want to be a pencil. I want to be a piece of paper. I want to
be a ruler. I want to be thin air.

GRASS.

Grass is here to make the world look beautiful.
Grass is soft…so that when we fall over, we don't get
hurt.
Grass is green because it suits the ground.
Rain cannot come out of grass that's why grass is not in
the sky…
Gods up in the sky,
On one of those clouds, on all of them…
Wherever you imagine he is…
He is.

LIFE.

I was NOT brought by a bird they call a stork!
I was put by God in mummies tummy
I was born when I was none days, none years old.
I will grow up and get a ring…
Wedding ring,
Get in love
And there's children following behind.

STORY TIME.

WRITTEN WITH THE HELP OF THE OLDER
CHILDREN WHO CHOSE KEY WORDS FOR THE
YOUNGER CHILDREN TO REPEAT OUT LOUD AS
THE STORY PROGRESSED. [The words would be
written on the board and pointed at when arrived at in the
story].

It was that kind of day when eggs and bacon could be
fried on pavements, [SIZZLE SIZZLE] and roads had
their best chance of melting motorcar tyres [STICKY
STUCK RUBBER]. It was that time of day when clocks
chimed a top score, [TING TING TING TING TING
TING TING TING TING TING TING TING] and offices
licked their lips [do action] and bellies asked for food
[GURGLE GURGLE].
The teacher wiped his forehead [do action] PHEW he
went, IT'S SO HOT! As he got to the school, he felt in his
jacket pocket [RUSTLE RUSTLE] for his keys [JINGLE

74

JINGLE]. He placed the key in the lock [RATTLE RATTLE] and turned the key [CLICK].

Although today was a Friday all the children had a holiday [HOORAY HOORAY] and the teacher could hear some of the children down the road laughing [HA HA HA HA] as they enjoyed their extra day away from school [YIPEEEEEE]. The teacher however had to come in to do some extra work [AHHHHH POOR POOR TEACHER]. As he entered his classroom he shivered [BRRRRRRR] although the whole classroom was bathed in sunlight…it felt freezing cold [SHIVER SHIVER]. Between the empty chairs he could hear yesterday's voices whispering [WHISPER WHISPER] from empty table to empty table. Suddenly he noticed on his desk a big black box sitting there all alone just yelling to be opened [OPEN ME OPEN ME].

He slowly walked to his desk, so quietly you could hear his new shoes squeak [SQUEAK SQUEAK].

The school building was so silent [HUSH HUSH] and so cold [BRRRRRRR] you could hear his bones creak and crack [CREAK CREAK CRACK CRACK].

Keeping his eyes all the time on the big black box, he sat down very slowly as if his legs and the chair legs were made of eggs!

Carefully he pulled the big black box towards him…it was heavy. He pulled it to the edge of his desk…he was now looking directly over the top of it. His breathing was heavy, [HEAVY HEAVY] he could hear his heart thumping quickly [THUMP-THUMP THUMP-THUMP THUMP-THUMP THUMP-THUMP]. He saw the lid had hinges and that to open it he would have to lift it from the front. Gently he held the sides and moved the lid up a centimetre or two…he put an ear to the tiny gap and listened…nothing. He lifted the lid up a couple more centimetres…he looked…only darkness. He knew he had to open it quickly, all at once, and just look in!

Don't be silly, don't be a big baby he said to himself, if my class could see me now…their big strong fearless teacher scared of a…of a…?

Right, I'll count to 3 then lift up the lid and look straight down inside…right to the bottom of the box!

ONE…somethings moving!

TWO…it's going to be something horrible I know!

TWO AND A QUARTER, TWO AND A HALF, TWO AND THREE QUARTERS,

NO THIS IS SILLY

THREE! LID UP

FACE FULL OVER

LOOKING DOWN INSIDE…

ARRRRRGHHHHH OOOOOOOO…YELLS THE TEACHER!!!

[The children were asked if they could guess what was so scary inside? My answer…A scary reflection…it was a mirror!].

RIDDLE ONE.

I am very small.
Have wings and I am a she.
There are loads of me.
We all live in heaven in the sky.
We go there when we die.
We make rain,
God makes sunshine.
We come down to earth in blobs of rain.
We land on the ground; the rain carries on underground.
If it's not under your pillow I'll give you nothing.

RIDDLE TWO.

There is space in which plastic air can go anywhere. If it
goes too far it is brought back to face the metal bars going
up and down.
The oblong can be made of anything, can have a slope but
better flat and not too hard.
No-one must use their hands, except those with warm
hands, then two hands are counted as one.
Anyone can watch.
It's the worms least favourite game, and a matter of life
and death for low-flying birds.
IT'S A GREAT GAME.

[Helping children turn their descriptions into riddles]
ANSWERS…
RIDDLE ONE a tooth fairy.
RIDDLE TWO a game of football.

WHEN I'M OLD ENOUGH!

I've fallen in love, head over heels in love…
I know I've only met her a few times, but it WAS love at
first sight!
She is beautiful…got lovely eyes full of love for me…
She likes the same food as me…chocolate, crisps, ice
cream,
And we play so well together…hang about on climbing
frames,
Rough and tumble gently in the grass.
Yes, there is no doubt about it…WE ARE IN LOVE!
One day when I'm old enough,
I don't care what anybody says…
I'm going to marry my monkey.

TREES THAT TALK.

Someone told me trees can talk, so next day I went to see
a tree and found an oak tree. I stood next to it and
listened…NOTHING!
After a few minutes I said, 'Hello tree, I was told that you
could talk to me!' SILENCE.
Then…its branches stretched to the skies gently waving
and swaying.
Its leaves flickered and rustled.
Its huge trunk creaked and cracked and its roots
Scratched and clawed deep underground.
I stood still saying nothing…
What do you think the tree said to me?
[OUCH?]

UNKIND LOVE.

I gave my dog a whole treacle tart
           a packet of chocolate biscuits
           a jar of peanut butter
           a packet of hedgehog flavoured crisp
I gave my dog half my dinner
I gave my dog an early death.

NUMBERS [Please tell me when I can stop].

One sunny day a beautiful one met a handsome one and
got married
On the first day of the first month in the first year, at
exactly one minute past one.
After three months short of one year, they made another
one…
Who grew up to meet another one
And they made another one
Who grew up to meet another one
And they made another one
Who grew up to meet another one
And they made another one
Who grew up to meet another one
And they made another one
[and so on until…].

THIS BOY IS UP THIS BOY IS DOWN
[How did he get there?].

A pink elephant on a purple skate board came rattling and rolling down the street. The boy had to quickly jump UP out of the way…
UNFORTUNATELY, he jumped and landed in a supermarket shopping trolly which began rolling DOWN the hill 10, 20, 30 miles per hour, 40 miles per hour…all the boy could do was HANG ON, 50, 60, 70 miles per hour, and right at the bottom of the hill he saw a policeman directing traffic…the boy covered his eyes…80, 90, now a hundred miles per hour!
SMACK BANG CRASH into the policeman, both catapulted UP into the air, 'I'll arrest you for this,' said the policeman somersaulting in mid-air.
DOWN DOWN they went, UNFORTUNATELY…they both landed on telephone wires…TWANG as back UP they both went flying high into the sky, through clouds UP…UP…UP…and then DOWN…DOWN…DOWN…
UNFORTUNATELY, as they were dropping DOWN a very low flying aeroplane flew underneath them both…the boy landed on one wing and the policeman landed on the other wing…
And they both went DOWN UNDER!

A STORY WITH A MORAL MESSAGE.

Many years ago, as I was walking in the forest a strange
thing happened. It was early in the morning before the sun
woke up and birds began yawning.

Deep in the darkened forest I could hear a strange
rumbling noise like distant thunder. This grumbling noise
seemed to come from one place in the forest so I crept
towards the noise that grew louder and louder, then
suddenly…it stopped.

Behind a bush I saw a large space with no trees, just a flat
open space surrounding a large hill, and in it I saw the
biggest collection of rounded objects I'd ever seen! There
were footballs, beachballs, netballs, tennis balls, even golf
balls and they were all surrounding this hill. On the side of
the hill was a square looking object in the shape of a
cardboard box and was painted in all different colours and
I realised it looked like it was made of plastic…yes it
definitely wasn't a cardboard box.

There was silence and all was still…Suddenly a voice
spoke…'We are all gathered here today to decide what
should be done with this object that says it is a square ball!
A square ball I ask myself…have you ever seen anything
look so silly as this object that thinks it's a square ball! I
say there is no such thing as a square ball. If it were meant
to be a ball it would be shaped round like all of us. I mean
this object can't even roll down a hill, look how its stuck
on the side of one such hill. It can't roll along the ground
smoothly, nor can it bounce without catching its edges on
the ground and wobble to a halt! It just can't bounce
anywhere. You should be a box or a building brick!'
Another voice shouted, 'I think we should destroy this
square that calls itself a ball.'

'Yes,' shouted another, 'Let's pierce it with a red-hot
needle…waggle the needle about until all its insides are

outside then throw it on the fire and watch it melt to nothing!'

A different voice, 'Light the fire, heat the needle... square have you any last words?'

'Well...well,' stuttered the square ball.

'Come on speak up, is the needle hot enough yet?

The square ball at last found the courage to speak, 'I know I am a different shape from all of you but I didn't choose to be this way I was just made this way. I know I can't roll as good as you or bounce as you can but I can do other things that you rounded objects can't do.'

There was silence...'Like what?' came a voice.

'Well, I can sit on a head all day without falling off and on the slope of this hill no rounded object could stay still like I can and wherever I'm placed I can stay and not roll away.'

'Let's have a vote,' cried a voice, 'If you think this object should be pierced with a red-hot needle then thrown on the fire then bounce once. If you think this object should be allowed to live as a square ball then bounce a million times!'

BLIBBA BLABBA BLUBBA.

Somewhere I hear a garden gate BURST open!
And my ears prick up to pick up a…
BLIBBA BLABBA BLUBBA sound.
I run to my bedroom window…
And looking out I pick out a…
Huge fat slimy green dripping blob of a creature!
Gripping my bedroom curtain in shock horror of the
moment…
The sound reaches the backdoor downstairs…
BLIBBA BLABBA BLUBBA!
Roughly translated means…EYZER-COMIN-TER-GET-
YERRRRRRRRRRRR!
My stomach in my throat, my heart in my ears, I sprint to
open my bedroom door…
[The bathroom the only place to lock myself in.]
Out on the stairs…
I feel a presence…
BLIBBA BLABBA BLUBBA!
Too late, no use, no chance, as suddenly the creature sucks
me into its hold…
I shriek, THIS-AS-GOTTA-BE-A-NIGHTMARE!
As it gobbles me up…
Bone by bone…
MUNCH MUNCH
CRUNCH CRUNCH
SCRUNCH SCRUNCH
YUMMY YUMMY YUMMY…
Now who's going to be the next one for MEEEEEEEEE!!!

WRITTEN ON A COMMUTER TRAIN
AFTER READING T.S. ELIOTS WASTE LAND.

She sits alone in a room
Tapping her keys out in time
While she sits at home
Watching the T.V. soaps
And copes with another day.
Come now away day
As in the same carriage
A different look,
a worn away.
A man reading the Sports page turns to me,
Shows an advert on the golf page…
Dead or alive, trying to tell him something, mentions
about his wife
Counting pebbles on the shore, my thoughts not his words.
The closeness of bodies
Each routine huddled together
Knees accidently touching knees
Quick glances
Body heat rising to pitch the absurd
Still no words
Took four years to talk to her fellow commuters,
Well…mornings are hell…who wants to talk?
And evenings spent resenting time on the line,
Grinding away,
Week-ends just a snip to put in what's gone…
All in a day
A day's work
A day's work never ends.

October haze, sun sinking the light
All lights off as the eyes look down
Then up to faces passing outside the window,

Back down again
Dreaming of the future
Rolling a dead thought.

One more platform
One more name
Bip-bip-bip-bip empty spaces
Matching still vacant faces
Words could not leap the gap to match
The one thought of a disaster
A sharing of a moment
When humanity clings together,
Caring the experience
Chasing the warmth after the glow
One more platform
On your marks, get, set…go!

Mrs Marple at number 62
Hangs out her washing at 9 o'clock every day
Saturday bingo,
Sunday church never misses a note,
Her old man still wears his medals
A proud chest stripped of everything else
Any different eating from a tin can?
Or a cardboard cut-out?
Home for some.
These two worked hard
For their two-up-two-down terraced house,
Suits them down to their Sunday best
Until that day he messed the sheets.

The tracks go up
But also go down
In dear old London town.
Salute the bustling capital

Money magnet mountains
Coffee coloured nightmares
A business brain,
Feeding the computer screen brightly the night,
Tired eyes rubbed, scrubbed of life
All in a day's work, working for the government,
Supporting the system
Bip-bip-bip-bip
Let me out he screams
Get me off he shrieks…
Faces turn on him
And smirk
An umbrella covers the emergency chain
You're stuck here like all of us
And if you don't make a fuss no-one will know, you
know.

The river glideth at its own pace
Remarkable how nature survives
When faced with adversity,
The tug boat knows where the tide lies
It feels its way
Choppy still
It feeds its will with nature
Nature
Nature to reel in the past
Unhook it, chuck it back in
Skin and all.
Looking back at the bridge, he's appalled
At what he's seen in the space of 5 miles
Either side of St. Pauls.
Tickets please
Anyone please, double quick
Show me an open face, before I'm sick.

'Who are you?'
'Who ARE you?'
'I asked first, please answer! Who are you?'
'Who? I am you!'
'Don't be clever.'
'I'm not, I AM you.'
'You can't be.'
'Why not?'
'Because I'm asking the questions.'
'No! You've asked me a question now I'll ask YOU
one...Who are you?'
'Well...That's a good question.'
'I know it is...Well?'
'Well...I suppose I must be you.'
'Just as I said!'

Work at life! And we do!
Smile at life! Oh, that's not so easy
Difficult when the capital's sun
Hides behind mid-morning mist,
She kisses her son good-night Sunday and
Says hello to him Saturday morning.
Work at life and they do
Her son will grow-up never getting to know his father
Missing the gaps in each silence
Ignoring the eyes, talking to the mouth
Hugs outside the window,
But he's a man and he'll make it,
Had a good role model
Work at life and he will
Snapshot...still life
Negatives developed to support the race
Keep pace, keep pace
Please mind the gap.

Chasm
The chasm
Falling between two edges
Each fatal, each jagged as eyes
Pricked into existence by an urge
Which way?
The necessity to produce? What? Why?
Make way for the romantic age
Blank page
Empty words
Invisible ties
Old school know what I mean old bean?
Don't fight the system
Go with the flow
You'll be alright
You can count on me old boy.

In the garden she cultivates
The smell of memories,
Each one cascading each experience
In front of her eyes,
Smiling at the scent of all occasions
Silence
The bird's song
Sheep bleat
Spring is here again
Silence
All open to hope, all pointing to disappointment
In what?
Romantic dogma?
Commercial tricksters?
Or to her, happy in her silence…
He could be humming along
Strumming the day in perfect consolidation
Thinking he can be whoever he wants to be,

See, there he goes hooking a snatch
Of creation
Living freely
Chasms
Nurtured selfishly?
Or selflessly?

WRITINGS
FROM A FATHER TO HIS SON.

[1]

Standing 58 years old with a pregnancy test in my hand…
And in those few minutes
Between showing nothing,
Or growing a world of wonder…
And then the two blue lines
Next day to confirm…one more test…same result…
YOU… MY SON!

[2]

Joking with your mother about it being an immaculate
conception!
And if it's a boy and he's born on Christmas day…
We will have to call him Jesus and change our names to
Mary and Joseph…
Welcome the son of God then…
Seriously I say to myself if there truly is a God…
Then…thank-you God
For this precious gift of a child.

20th July 2011.

Taking the bus to the hospital, both excited to know the sex…
The woman asks, 'Do you want to know?'
We both say, 'Yes,' in harmony…
'It's a boy,' she says.
And my eyes fill up with tears.
Then all the checks…but no…you had to be independent, your own boss?
Or just plain awkward? YOU in the wrong position to check your heart, so…
Out we went and told to walk upstairs up and down and then back into the ultrasound…
No good…so outside we went again then back inside…Still no good…
Out again this time up and down a hill…Then your position ok…all good.
I smiled as it began to rain as we walked to the bus, laughing that maybe you were playing with us so we would get wet?
Your mother said that I had told you to behave on the last walk otherwise you won't be getting any pizza!
As off we went to Pizza Hut in the Marina
For a celebration of your identity
No longer a baby
But now…James Nathan Blackman.

●●●●●●●●●●●●●●●●●●●●●●●●●●●●●●●●●●●

So, if you were alive today
And I could ask you how do you wish to be delivered?
Normal birth or caesarean?
What would you decide?
Not care? As long as you come out alive?
But oh, think of your parents and what they would have to
go through!
No, of course it's none of your worry…
All you're thinking about is your next breath…
That's it, James…just breathe.
When we look back on the 3 months when we didn't know
you were growing…
We wonder how you managed to 'hang on in there' inside
of mummy's tummy,
What with her doing vigorous exercises on a leg machine
in Hove Park and…
Showing your mother all corners of Paris!
But what could we do?
We thought we were not to be blessed,
Thought missed periods were the start of the menopause…
But then the positive test…
The realisation, the wonder, the miracle,
The gift from the universe
From God?

6th September 2011.

With the wind and rain
Making its presence felt outside
While inside I stand by the modern-day fire
Boiling my egg
And then bending down to peel its shell
I feel its perfection,
Its beauty, its function,
And standing up I thought all in my world is perfection,
And turning to the thought of you James…
Made me think…I don't know what sort of father I will be
to you?
But what I am sure of is that I will share my sense
Of wonder of the world
And with my eyes and yours
We will explore
The beauty that life
Presents…
All this stemming from
Shelling an egg
What small beginnings…
What huge outcomes!

14th February 2012.

Taking over the night shift you watch your mummy
disappear into the other room,
Then you come back into your milky world, head still on
one side close to my knees
Your back resting on my upper legs bent up…
You continue feeding until nearing the emptying of the
bottle you begin to act drunk,
Cheeks full, eyes heavy, you finally sleep a deep
wonderful sleep, your mouth still open
From when daddy withdrew the bottle…you sleep deep,
snoring and I watch you for 15 to
20 minutes till suddenly you awake, seem startled as if
coming into a big world…
And wondering where you are? Me pondering where
you've been in your sleep?
I massage your toes, as your eyes focus firstly on
me…how you study me as if looking
Deep inside me, peering into my soul. You look at me
then smile a wide smile, you gurgle,
I smile, I giggle…you try to communicate yet seem
obstructed without a vocabulary, yet
Still, you try as for 15 minutes we exchange different
expressions, smiles and noises…
I lift you up and say, 'How long your legs are.' I get you
to stand on your feet on my chest,
'Oh, how very tall you are,' I say…you chuckle, gurgle,
laugh as you look down on me then
Shriek as if joyful at stretching your body and the feeling
of putting your whole
Weight on your legs,
Up and down, we go
Until suddenly from laughter to crying…
Tired…back to sleep

This time your chest on my bare chest
Head snuggled in
Dummy in mouth
Another bonding-sleep.

A SYMPATHY SYMPHONY.

What a smile!
A smile that could melt
A thousand hearts
But oh, when he begins
To whimper then cry
So that his bottom lip begins to quiver…
IT MAKES MY HEART BLEED
And from his symphony
It creates sympathy
And my song…
'My poor-poor James please don't cry [cwy]…
I don't like it when you cry [cwy]…
Yes, I know, I know, you poor-poor boy…
No, please don't cry [cwy].'
And so, on and on
And on…until…
His bottom lip stops quivering
Still remaining low down
Until returning to…
Oh, what a smile!!!

KILLIE-KILLIE [TICKLE TICKLE].

Nappy change…
On the bed…
Bare bottom…
You look at me…
You wait…
I move towards you…
You begin to open your mouth…
I reach down…
And tickling your bottom…
KILLIE-KILLIE I go…
As off you go huge smile…
Giggle-giggle
What fun
One more game
One more interaction.

Monday 25th June 2012.

James perhaps one day in your adulthood,
When you find yourself in a posh restaurant…
With a sophisticated young lady,
And she says to you, 'Choose whatever you want, it's my treat.'
And through nothing more than instinct you immediately
Say, 'Salmon, oh yes salmon please.'
She says, 'What smoked?'
'Just salmon,' you say, 'And with a lovely sauce…yoghurt.'
She says, 'Really?'
'Yes,' you say, 'Raspberry flavour.'
And James you can blame your parents who on Monday 25th June 2012 gave you your first
Salmon mashed up and you didn't like it, maybe because we made the mistake of giving
You your yoghurt before, so we mixed the salmon with raspberry yoghurt…yum-yum no
Problem…you ate it all…
And in that restaurant remember to tell her about Monday

25th June 2012.

THE GRAND TOUR.

His Royal Highness Prince James enjoys nothing more than a tour around his stately home…First to the kitchen, the big white machine that gives us hot water and heating…He studies…then the sink, I run the water…He studies…then the pots and pans and plates drying…He touches, then holding in his sitting position back upright he looks out the kitchen window…'That's the world out there,' I say and he watches the people go by and the leaves on the trees move around in the summer breeze. Back to the kitchen and the cooker, then to the cupboards, and now nearly 6 months old he opens one door and looks at all the different shapes and sizes and colours…I rattle one container of gravy granules then he closes the door. I show him the washing machine going round and round…He studies…Then looks at me…'Yes my Prince I am your loyal servant giving you all you need,' as to the lounge we go and a panoramic view as I circle the T.V. the computer…the sofa until we get to the map of the world on the wall and I point saying, 'This is where you live and this is where mummy comes from…look at the distance between,' as I draw a line with my finger as he measures the distance into his future as I say. 'Mummy came a long way to have you.' We move onto the paintings, then the cupboards full of clothes, then to the window and drawing back the curtain he sees the world outside as again he looks at me…'Yes I'm here,' I say, 'It's a big place out there.' Then we go to the bedroom only allowed to visit in the afternoons because of the sleeping Queen Mother royally snoring her crown off and then to the bathroom where he comes face to face with himself…He smiles and laughs.

SWEET BABY JAMES.

Oh James…sweet baby James, how much your weight has
changed…
Although only seven and a half kilos you feel heavier than
a ten-kilo bag of rice [which
many times, I have carried.]
So why the difference?
Maybe the rice didn't move when carried?
Oh, my back, my poor back…how I wish your mother
would let me carry YOU on my head.
WHAT A SENSE OF HUMOUR.

SCREAM.

During a few weeks you began a screaming phase,
And trying to teach you not to do this
I was having some success and then
When one time I said, 'JAMES NO SCREAMING.'
You opened your mouth and screamed very quietly…
What a performance…
Never again did you scream a loud scream…
GOOD BOY.

23rd January 2013.

How important it will be I do not know,
But trusting my instincts I will let the future
Unravel its answers as I spend time with my 14-month-old
son in play…
In play with just him and me in a room, in a space
Playing loudly, playing gently with his selection of toys
Having experiences like the other day with me lying down
fascinated by one of his toys,
He eyeing me while he plays with his toy,
And for the first time I notice he doesn't take my toy away
from me
But continues in our moment of experience, of sharing.
How important this will be in his development time will
tell
A moment not to waste, a particular event
In the life of a small child and his father…
A time I will never forget.
HOLDING HUGS.

DIFFERENT PERSPECTIVE.

One of the countless things my spirit has created
Is the holding of my son James in my arms up on one
shoulder,
Usually, my right
Feeling him hugging my neck...
He sometimes shrieks with delight
Other times his mother observing...
His smiling, his feeling superior
And when she asks me why he looks so proud
I say because I am giving him a different perspective...
Think how his life is mostly crawling
Often looking up
Always having a view of life low down flat no elevation
But when I hold him aloft
He can see the whole room, see the layout expand
Even the outside view is available through the window
And when I walk up and down
He has this outlook on his surroundings just as an adult
And for this
He is happy
For this
He is grateful
In his own way
In his hugs
And shrieks.

WHAT WILL YOU BE?

So, when I see you interested in
The binding of a book
I think you may become a bookbinder.

When I see you examine your racing car
With such involvement
Will you be a mechanic?

And when I hear you make your
Brrrr brrrr brrrr noises
I wonder if you will be a truckdriver?

And when I place you on a swing
In the park playground
Squealing with excitement
I think you're just a baby
Experiencing life
And who knows what you will become
Whatever you will be
I just hope
You will continue
To show to your mother and me
That you are genuinely, wholeheartedly
HAPPY.

26th February 2013.

I remember the first time you stood up on your own
Unknowingly whilst watching T.V.
I remember the first time you gave me a big hug
In my arms walking the lounge.
I remember the first time you gave mummy a kiss
Open mouthed wet saliva copying daddy.
I remember the first time you gave me a kiss
Crawling across the bed in our playing sessions.
I remember the first time you shared our humour together
Blowing raspberries together both laughing.
I remember these first times
But am now waiting for the first time
When you walk on your own doing more than just a few
steps,
When you talk words understood by your parents…
Take your time my son…
You have the rest of your life,
Just be happy in your state
That's all I ask…
All I wish.

A VARIATION ON A THEME.

In your buggy we head for the museum gardens where I
let you out close to the benches and instead of
investigating these...
You head off, arms balancing, legs quickening towards
your goal...
Under the trees to the gate...and the signs.
Finding them you point, then look back at me, arms open
and upwards.
I play a game with you by running away in slow motion...
You quickly catch me and holding my hand you lead me
back to the gate and the signs.
Picking you up you pull up my hand as if instructing me to
say what the sign says.
I point to each word and speak it and you listen, and you
touch everywhere,
Until I let you down and you're off round the corner,
down the side onto the grass
Tap dancing on the drain cover then onwards to the
museum entrance,
And the doors and the squeal and the enjoyment, then
down the slope, up the slope,
Down the steps, up the steps, back to the doors, then out to
the main entrance by the road
Bu-bu-bu, then another sign to lift you up to explain, then
outside on the pavement by the
Road, another sign to lift you to read, then still in my arms
a big-big-bus, then another
Then one more, you watching them every centimetre of
the way, until no more
And I put you back in your buggy, unclipped to send you
back to where we began by
The benches as once again off you go running free...
Running wild.

15th October 2013.

Having had a good morning doing our usual circuit in the
buggy
Going at snail pace so James can observe all his
surroundings
And then back to the flat I say wait for me while I put the
buggy away,
So you can have a walk…wait for daddy… and you do
and then all done…
Off you go-go-go and you set off out onto the pavement
letting you decide
Which way to go left or right? You choose right observing
all the lumps and cracks
Getting to the road you reach your hand out for my hand,
well trained, now we cross the
Big road…
Then down to your new assault course outside the
surgery…steps, curbs, grass, ramps,
All there to test your balance, give you confidence and
you gain it in abundance
As off we go along the pavements stopping at all your
favourites…
The chained railings
The numbers on certain houses,
Asking to be lifted at different signs…me reading, you
listening…
Then home for your milkies and lying-in bed starting your
mid-day sleep
Your milk finished, me patting you to sleep…you point
your finger to touch
The tip of my nose, me trying not to laugh, you seeing the
laughter swelling up in my eyes until I have to let it
out…you laugh a natural sharing laugh,

And then I touch your nose the same way and we both
laugh a hearty laugh
Sharing
And forging a simple special moment
One of so many I'm certain...
You just living in the moment
Enjoying one more priceless moment.

28th January 2014.

These moments of innocence…brushing a stick into a puddle,
Then stroking it on the pavement,
Feeling the shape of metal formed gates,
Touching the early flower of the year…and smelling…
And so, we venture inside to your joy of joining me under a blanket our own cave tunnel
And you lie there for one moment, feet and hands exploring the roof of our hideaway,
And squealing when you return to our reality of play.
And then another moment when giving you a biscuit you remind me of being an adult
As I hold it in one hand eating it, while you hold separate pieces in each hand munching
On one then another, scrunching on both at the same time…simple things made different…
What lessons learnt. I wish you to know James how much my love has grown for you…
Your smile…Your innocence, your vulnerability, your creativity.
I love to see you smile whether it's when we play or when you give me your toy car,
Expecting me to understand what you want me to do like turning the switch to hear it
Speak and when it does your joy…your smile at what you wished exactly to happen…
Yes, I love your adventure, your gradual understanding of your world, of language,
Of life.
So much to grasp, yet there is time and I am aware
There will be plenty of it…
No rush…no pressure…you carry on learning my son…you enjoy

No testing…no assessment…no score…
Just play…keep enjoying your happiness,
Your smile the true indicator of whether as a parent we are getting it right.

April 2014.

PART 1.

It was a Saturday morning when we were outside the shop, the Fire shop
After coming down the alleyway and no cycling, and outside the shop
You pointed to the no smoking sign and said, 'No poo.'
At first, I didn't connect with this but the second time you said it I did, then
After the third time you pointed and said, 'No poo,' I looked up to the sky or heavens
And said, 'Grand tat are you watching? That is what you his great grandfather said for a smoke…a poo. How could my son understand that? Are you watching over us? Are you all watching?'
'No poo,' he says
I have never taught him that
No-one could ever make that connection
I have never mentioned it to him,
It has to be you my dear Grand tat, you that gave me so much attention,
So much love
What a connection
What a feeling of the spirit
And each time my son said it,
It joined me with all my family…
My grandparents
My parents
My family
Thank-you all, thank-you James
For connecting me with my ancestors
And your family James.

PART 2.

And so, we found ourselves outside the same shop
In the same road
And I pointed to the no smoking sign
And you looked at me James full faced, and smiled a
cheeky smile
And I smiled at you Grand tat, your great grandad,
I laughed with you Grand tat through your great grandson
And we became closer
And confirmed
The generations link
With you
My dear parents and grandparents
Thank-you James
For bringing our family
Back together
Again.

September 2014.

And during one more evening sharing your playtime, your
milk time,
You're watching CBeebies time, we come to the end of
the Night Garden…
'Charlie Bear,' you exclaim. 'No let's watch the end, you
know Daddy likes to see Igglepiggle go off in his
boat'…so you agree without words and stand in front of
the T.V. just as the bridge, the grandstand, the flowers, the
house full of lights blend into the sky,
Now becoming stars as all merges into the universe and in
that moment, I feel, your mind,
Being melted into a feeling of awe…what a
word…wonderment…what an emotion…
A sense of AWE…I say it again as father and son share an
unconscious moment…thank you.
My boy and I return once more to that thought of how do I
want my son to turn out like?
Confident…compassionate
kind…caring…gentle…honest…tolerant…a sense of
being
A spiritual person…respecting others…remembering
peoples' weaknesses, aware of others
Individual battles…a feeling of responsibility to oneself,
not blaming others, being true
To oneself, understanding who you are and where you
came from…
Be a happy person my son…be a good man my flesh and
blood…
Remember me and your mother and our family line
And share this with your future.

June 2015.

Your mother at last more relaxed now your language is
growing,
Your mind ticking over nicely as I continue to exercise
your being
In more ways than one...your sense of humour
exchanging with mine.
Your excitement ignited by my emotion
Your confidence in the palm of my sensitivity
Your character allowed to run free at times in control for
safety...
Your kindness given chances to shine
Sharing a normal problem being worked on you...
You're doing well my son but most of all it pleases me to
see just how much you are
Enjoying your life, your beginning, your crucial first
FOUR YEARS.

July 2016.
UPON A NIGHT OF REFLECTION.

So, why my son have I not written to you for so long?
My answer is I have been watching you instead…
Fascinated by your development in so many ways…
Why would I want to write
When I am transfixed by your actions,
Your mannerisms,
Your innocence
Your learning
Your inner battles with the world and who you are…who
you will become.
I have watched and I have learnt from you my son…
I have learnt much more from you than you will ever
know
You my precious beautiful son who taught me once again
to be patient
To return closer to my Buddhist ways to exercise pure
compassion
And the most special of them all…
To live once more IN THE MOMENT,
IN THE HERE AND NOW
No past, no future only the seconds you are living in…
So precious so alive
Opening-up a face, a mouth, a smile.
Thank-you my son and in return a poem for you
A time when nothing is lacking and
Sharing a wonderful presence.

November 2016.
ONE MORE MOMENT.

Late November coming back from Abi's party
The one you didn't want to go into…
The environment not comfortable for you
So, we went to Portland Park
And pushing you back from there
To Pembroke Crescent we saw piles of fallen leaves
Along the pavement
So, sitting in your buggy
And like some huge snow machine
I ploughed full speed through each pile
And as each one was separated and spread
A huge mountain of leaves
Got stuck and piled up in front of your buggy
As one more heap split apart
Bigger the huge ball of leaves
As onward we strove
You laughing such a lovely laugh
And me joining in the laughter
Sharing, enjoying one more moment
When father and son were uncontrollably
AT ONE.

ANOTHER GAME.

Daddy. 'What is that?'
James. 'What is that?'
Daddy. 'No that.'
James. 'No that.'
Daddy. 'Are you copying me?'
James. 'Are you copying me?'
Daddy. 'Are you a parrot?'
James. 'Are you a parrot?'
Daddy. 'Give me lots of big-big kisses.'
PAUSE…SILENCE.
James. 'Give me lots of big-big kisses.'
Daddy. Mmmmmmmmmmm [lots of kisses all over
James as he laughs out loud.]

December 2016.

What is it?
Is it the beauty of his innocence?
Or the freshness of his five-year-old face?
What is it?
Is it the way he sometimes gazes at nothing
Lost in the moment
Or thinking in a simple way of a more complex thought
Not yet full of words?
What is it?
Is it the trusting nature in which he expects everything
from you
That your whole life should have taught you to give?
Or could it be something always out of reach?
No, it is much more than all of this.
What is it then?
It is the purest love
Both vulnerable and fulfilling
That places you in any situation every day
Of unconditional love
THAT IS WHAT IT IS.

March 2017.

FOR MY SON.

I love the way when we get close
And contact our bodies
You purr like a cat in contentment
As on my chest I hear you breathe deeper
And louder.

I love the way when you first wake up
And see me diving towards you
You with a sleepy smile
Open your arms to welcome me
Into your embrace.

I love the way when you are wanting
To have a game of something or do a play
You ask me out loud, 'Daddy can
We play?'

I love the way I love you my son
And I love your way
In so many more different ways
Thank-you.

April 2017.

ONE MOMENT IN PLAY
[When a 5-year-old connects with a 63-year-old.]

Yet one more storyline
This time Toy Story and an escape with a new twist…
Lotso the naughty bear is not accepted by the rest of the
Toy story gang
Because he betrayed them in the landfill site but James
brings him back into
The camp with a crocodile's mask over Lotso's head and
is accepted… except
Jessie, the cowgirl is not quite so sure and tells Woody
that this crocodile seems quite
Strange with his funny furry bear shape legs…
So…Woody and Jessie decide to test
This crocodile and agree that all bears love honey so if
when asked does he love honey,
If he answers NO then he must be a crocodile so…
Jessie asks the crocodile, 'Do you love honey?'
'NO,' he says but still Jessie is suspicious so she says to
Woody let's ask one more question to test if it is a
crocodile or if it is Lotso in disguise…every bear hates the
name Goldilocks because she ate their porridge etc so…
Jessie asks, 'Do you like the name Goldilocks?'
And the crocodile says, 'YES, I like the name.'
So, Woody says to Jessie, 'There we are, we have to
accept that he is a real crocodile with funny furry legs and
not Lotso in disguise.'
[But the smile you showed James when you went with the
story line was priceless!]

Spring 2020.

WHO ARE YOU?

Your mother continually asking…
What do you want to be?
After months of not answering the question
You finally say …
'I want to be me.'
Wow what an answer
[A Buddhist's answer?]

September 2023.
ANOTHER LEVEL.

Playdate number two…
Adult free
A moment in a parent's life
When they need to let go
A little?

Playdate number one…
The biggest worry?
Maybe not?
Dependent on how strong
The bond?

Playdates to come…
Building up to all-nighters?
Girlfriends, boyfriends not far away
The World at
Their feet?

Playdates for you to deal with
Now the adult…
Feel the necessity to trust
In your child whether they be
Wild or windy?
[windy… old slang for frightened]

HOPEFUL WISHING.

What would I wish from you my young son?
To listen carefully, openly, respectfully?
To observe all around you?
Be interested in everything?
Keeping hold of those areas your favourites?
Or is what I want inside of you?
A kindness
A thoughtfulness
An empathy of how humans can be,
How they can change, do change.
How you could be used, taken advantage of,
Knowingly or unknowingly.
For you to love
Be loved…now that is something we all want
And may you my dear son find it…
In a person who can see clearly your gifts,
Your humanity
And will treasure them and think on you as precious
As I your father thinks on you…
What I want from you my one and only child
Is for you to be happy both spiritually and emotionally
This is what I wish for you…
A hope.

REMEMBER THIS.

Remember this…
I will always be with you my son
Not just in the memories of your childhood and our games
We shared in countless joyful hours
That taught us so much about life and each other.

Remember this…
I will always be with you in other ways…
Like in the gentle sway of an old oak
It's leaves shining raindrops in the setting sun
Like in the flowers, I loved to sniff
In gardens on our many walks…this made you laugh.

Remember this…
I will always be with you even though physically
I will be far away but near enough
To be in your warmth, your kindness, your smile,
The tender, gentle ways you treat others…
I will be with you
As you will be with me
In my next life.

October 2023.
REACHING OUT.

What is it you want to say?
And why is it so important to say it?
Is it to do with you reaching 70?
Or the fact you are trying to allow the thoughts
To digest, to convey exactly what you need to
Obey?

Who is it that you want it read by?
And why is it so vital they feel it?
Is it to do with them reaching out
Or the fact, the simple fact of their thoughts
Accumulating to arrive at an understanding
Try?

So, I repeat what is it you are wanting to write about?
Love? Compassion? Spirituality?
Or a mixture of all? The seed has been planted
As carefully and thoughtfully as any father could do...
Take this page...keep it close...
And from time to time read it, feel it...
To know who I am
Who I was.

THE LAST POEM.

If this were to be my last poem,
I would write it to you
And you only because you have become
My focus, my goal, my mission.
After decades of freedom with few responsibilities
You came into my life to lengthen my living
Keeping away my death
By at least a couple of decades more for sure.
There is not one single regret I can think of but instead
You gave me the wonderful chance of taking all my years
in teaching
And my many relationships to put them into practice at
having a go at being a father!
Being someone, you could count on
Turn to.
Someone who would listen,
Love you always
Until…
And this is why I would write this for you
And you only…because
You gave me such joy and happiness
You gave me a perfect ending
To a long… long…life…
May you experience the same my son.
My dear loving son
Thank-you.

....

AUTHORS BIO.

Born in Hastings Ian left school at 16 to train as an accountant before finding his true vocation as a P.E. teacher.

At the age of 33 he began reading literature and poetry big time, inspiring him to write daily. He took the plunge to attend a week-long residential writing group with poet Carol Ann Duffy. He began poetry readings in schools and writing workshops under a Southern Arts Writers in Schools' scheme. He also spent a term in a Comprehensive school as a poet in residence, and a term in a junior/primary school. From these experiences he was able to run workshops not only to write about sport but also relationships.

Ian has lived in Sweden, Hampshire, Guernsey, Norfolk, Shropshire, Sicily, and on a Buddhist retreat in Essex, before returning to Sussex, where his son James lives.

He has published a novel, 'The Writes and Wrongs of a Wordplayer Manager,' as well as a collection of his poetry entitled 'Summer Rain.' [Both available on Amazon]. Another project on the horizon is a collection of wacky reports from Radio Skive Live's Sports reporter Ronnie Ranter whose character evolved from Ian's novel.

Printed in Great Britain
by Amazon